SATs Pra[ctice] in Maths

AGE 11

Rhona Whiteford and Jim Fitzsimmons
Illustrated by Sascha Lipscomb

The National Curriculum for England and Wales requires all 11 year-olds to be tested in English, Mathematics and Science. These tests are called SATs (Standard Assessment Tasks), and are completed during the normal school day. Their purpose is to give schools information about what children are achieving compared to others of the same age, and to highlight areas where help is needed. This book will help you to prepare your child for the SATs in Mathematics. Although the SATs are taken at age 11, this book may be used for practice throughout Year 6.

How to help your child

a Working together
If you work through each test with your child, you may discover areas where extra practice is needed.

b Test conditions
The SATs tests are timed at this stage, so you can use this book to prepare your child for real test conditions. Encourage them to work independently and with good concentration. Allow about 35 minutes for each test but do not be too strict about timing if your child is anxious. Do one test at a time, starting at the beginning of the book and working as far as you can through the three Test Groups (1-4, 5-8 and 9-11). Read each test together before your child starts to work through it.

Where it is necessary to work out a calculation, use a separate piece of paper as space is not available in this book. (It is in the SATs booklet.) In the SATs the calculation is sometimes marked too, so do go through the calculation with your child to make sure it is correct.

Children are allowed to use calculators in parts of the SATs, and 🖩 indicates points at which a calculator may be used in this book.

- Keep sessions short and frequent, perhaps one test per day.
- Make sure you and your child are relaxed and have a quiet place in which to work.
- Avoid putting your child under pressure.
- Build your child's confidence by offering plenty of praise and encouragement.

Hodder Children's Books

The only home learning programme supported by the NCPTA

Number

TEST 1

Look at these numbers. The dotted line joins pairs of numbers which have a difference of 8. Continue the dotted line to join another pair of numbers.

① ⑩ ⑱ ㉖ ⑪
⑦ ⑯----㉔ ⑤
⓪—⑧ ⑲ ⑬ ✓

Write +, −, × or ÷ in each circle to make the calculation correct.

② 6 × 8 = 48 ✓ ③ 32 ÷ 4 = 8 ✓ ④ 4 × 25 = 100 ✓
⑤ 12 + 12 = 24 ✓ ⑥ 6 ~~×~~ 9 = 54 ✓ ⑦ 56 ÷ 8 = 7 ✓
⑧ 44 ÷ 11 = 4 ✓ ⑨ 123 + 56 = 179 ⑩ 98 − 27 = 71

Write each of the numbers in the correct place in the sequence.

⑪ 301   323   310   150

| 120 | 150 | 205 | 276 | 301 | 304 | 310 | 323 |

Draw a ring round each number which can be divided exactly by 10.

⑫ – ⑭ (130) 26 45 (60) 12 (90) 87 ✓

Find 2 numbers which total 97. Draw a ring round each one.

⑮ 23 17 (49) 38 24 (48) ✓

NUMBER   TEST 1

This is a number square with some numbers missing. The numbers along each edge must add up to 60. Put each of these numbers in a circle to make the totals correct.

10   20   30   40

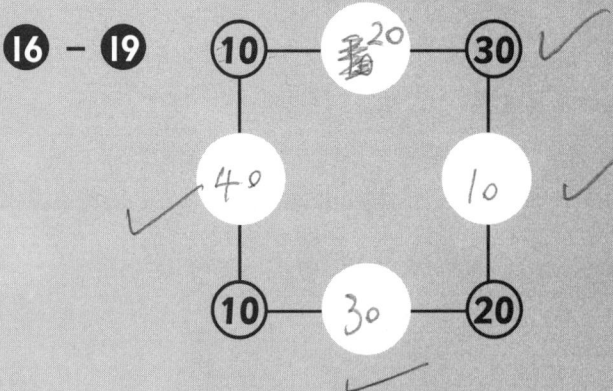

I think of a number. If I take away 25 it leaves 63. What is the number?

20   88

Write the missing numbers.

21
   5 4
+ 2 9
———
   8 3

22
   3 7
− 1 4
———
   2 3

23
   4 3
×   6
———
  2 5 8

24
   5 6
+ 3 6
———
   9 2

Complete each of these number lines by following the instruction.

25 3 less than	18	15	12	9	6	3
26 5 more than	10	15	20	25	30	35
27 multiply by 2	2	4	8	16	32	64
28 divide by 3	243	81	27	9	3	1
29 add 25	0	25	50	75	100	125

Excellent.

3

Shape, Space and Measures

TEST 2

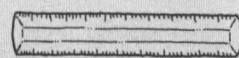

You will need: a ruler

Shapes **A** and **B** are squares. Shape **C** is a rectangle. Shapes **D** and **E** are triangles.

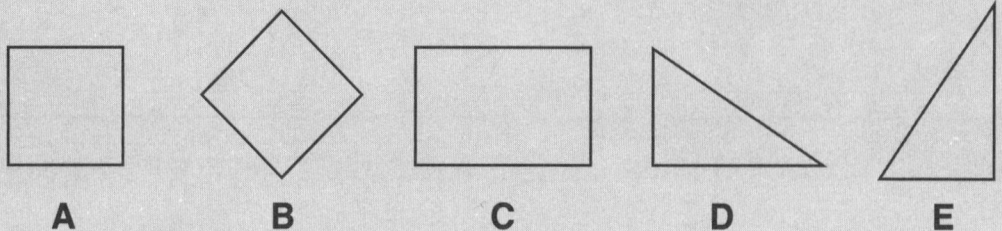

There are two ways in which all these shapes are alike. What are they?

① They've all got at least 1 right angle

② They've all got no reflex angles.

Use your ruler to measure the length of this pencil.

③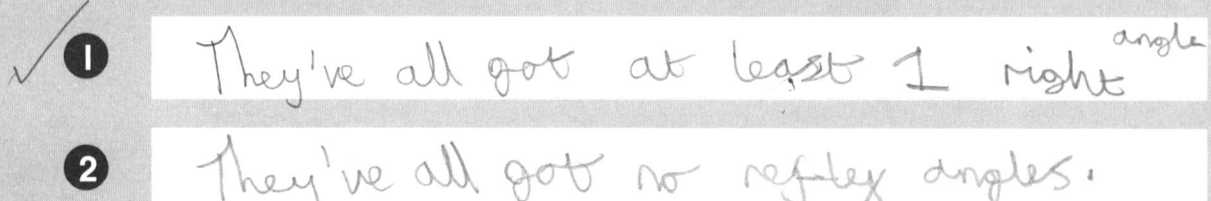

14 cm

Draw a line of symmetry on each of these letters.

④ ⑤ ⑥ ⑦ ⑧

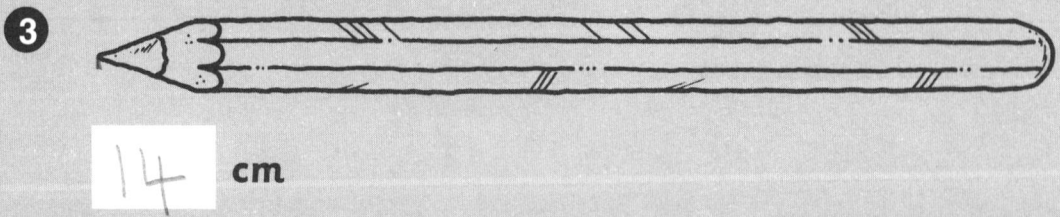

SHAPE, SPACE AND MEASURES   TEST 2

Put a tick ✓ under each obtuse angle. Put a cross ✗ under each acute angle.

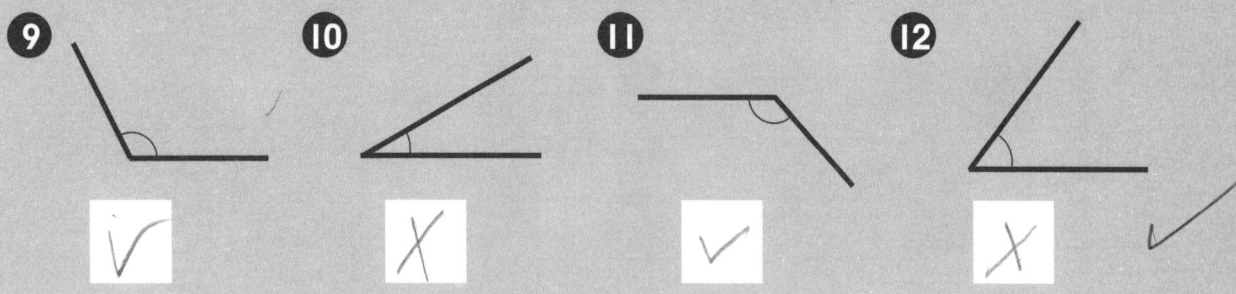

What is the perimeter of this rectangle?

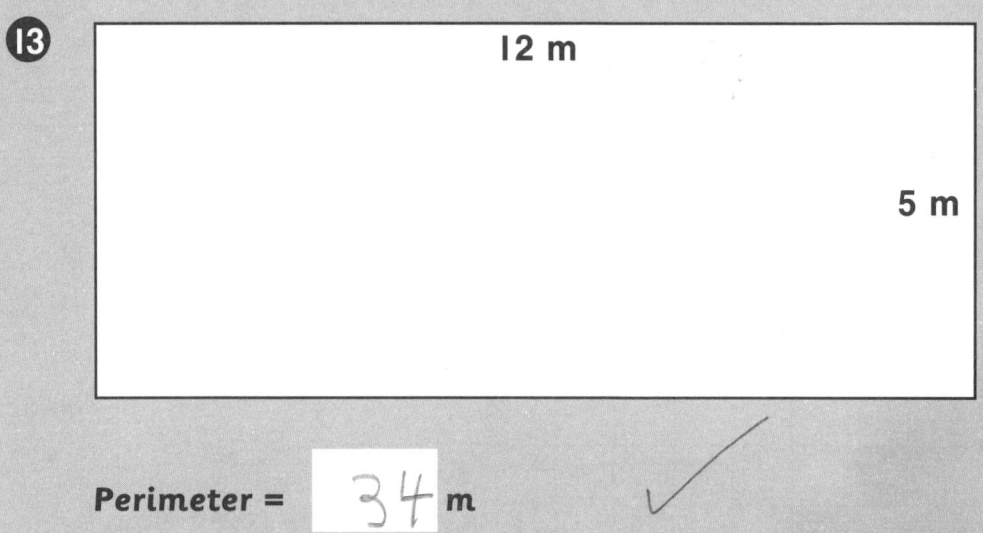

Perimeter = 34 m ✓

Here is a plan of a castle. What is the area of the tower (in squares)?

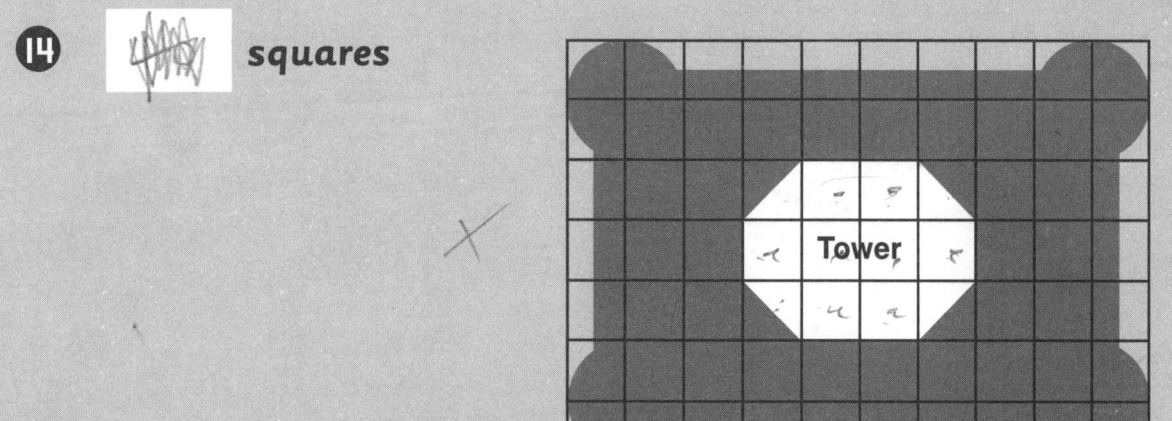

⑭ ~~4~~ squares

SHAPE, SPACE AND MEASURES   TEST 2

Shape **A** has a larger area than Shape **B**. Explain how you can work this out.

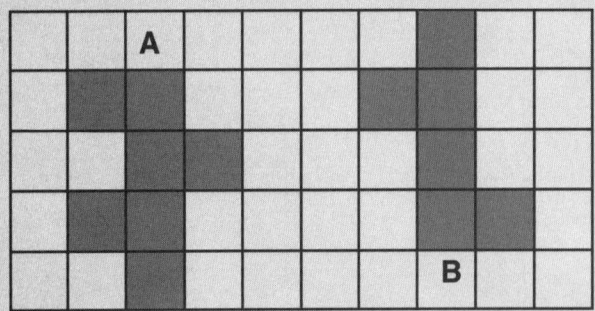

15 *You x the length by the breadth.* ✗

Look at Shape **C**. Draw another shape which has the same area.

16  ✓

This is a hexagon drawn on a circle.

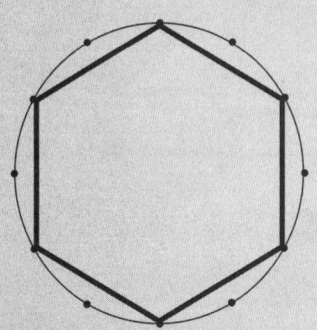

17 Draw an equilateral triangle on this circle. ✓

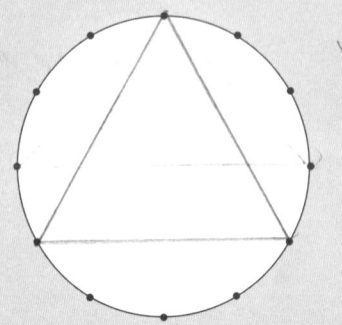

Handling Data

TEST 3

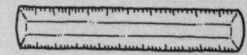

You will need: a ruler

This bar chart shows how many children had milk each day during one week.

❶ – ❹ Complete the chart using these figures.

DAYS OF THE WEEK	NUMBER OF CHILDREN
Monday	12
Tuesday	10
Wednesday	15
Thursday	18
Friday	9

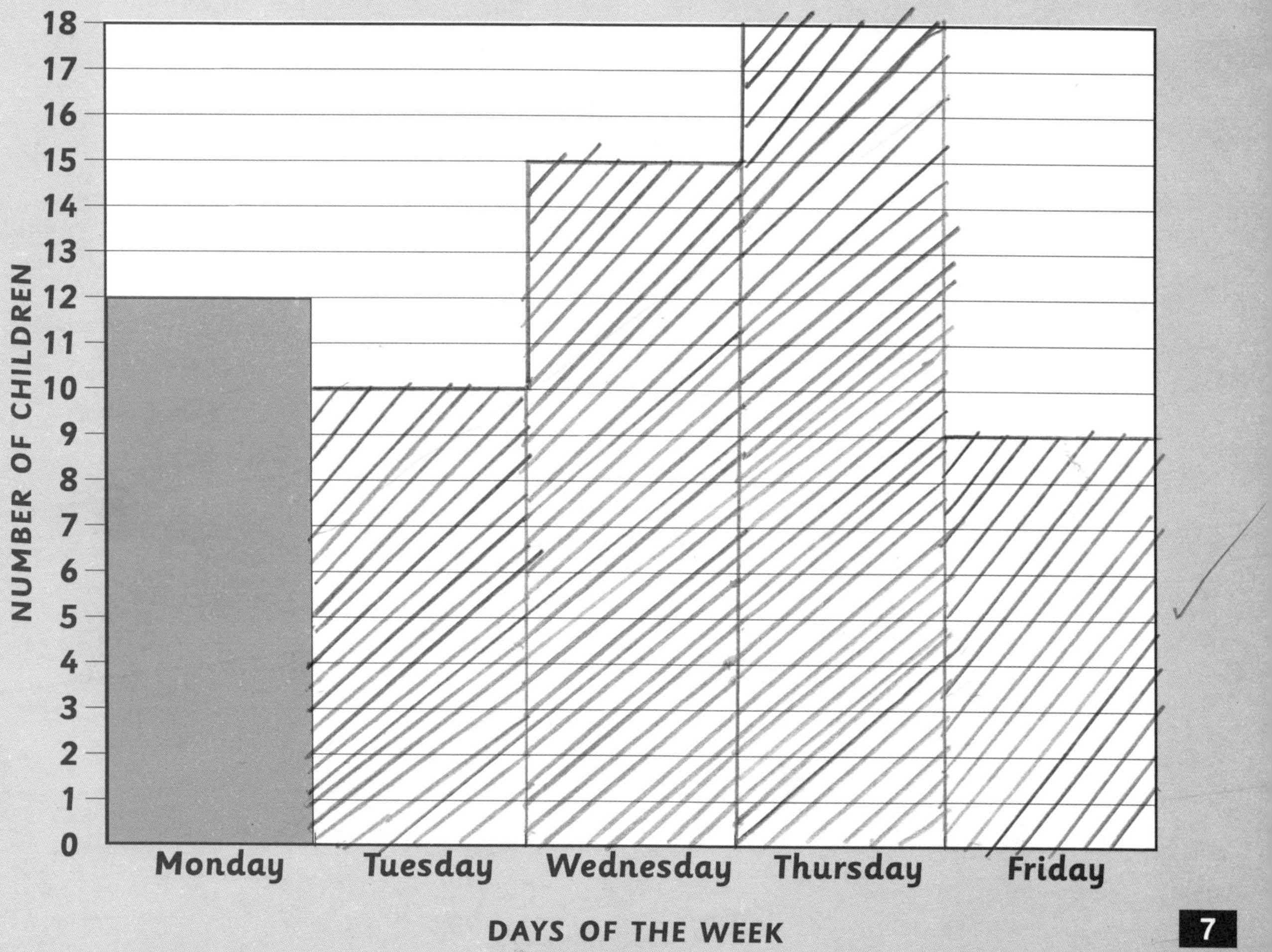

7

TEST 3   HANDLING DATA

This block graph shows the vehicles recorded in a traffic survey. Use the information to answer the questions.

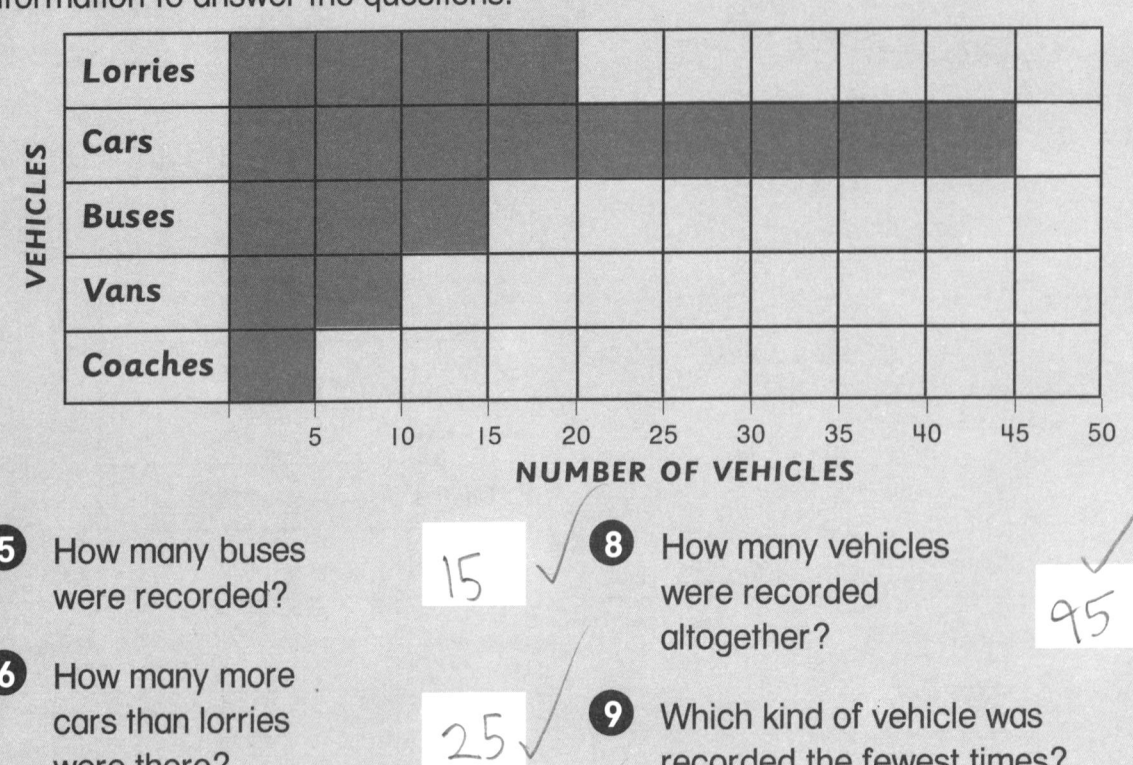

5 How many buses were recorded? 15 ✓

6 How many more cars than lorries were there? 25 ✓

7 How many fewer buses than lorries were there? 5 ✓

8 How many vehicles were recorded altogether? 95 ✓

9 Which kind of vehicle was recorded the fewest times? a Coach ✓

A group of children took part in a survey to find out their favourite television programmes. This pie chart shows the results.

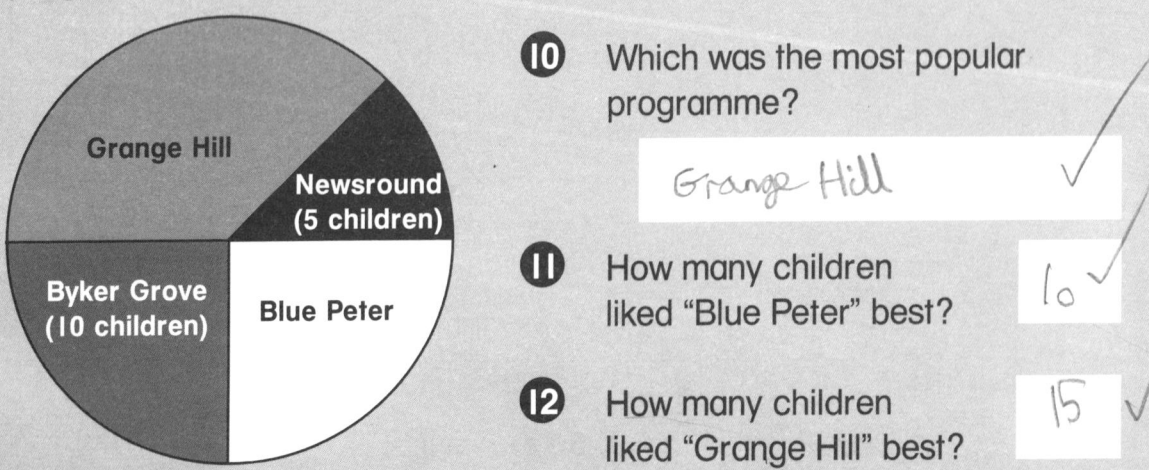

10 Which was the most popular programme? Grange Hill ✓

11 How many children liked "Blue Peter" best? 10 ✓

12 How many children liked "Grange Hill" best? 15 ✓

8

HANDLING DATA　　　　　　　　　　TEST 3

13　Which was the least popular programme?　　Newsround ✓

14　How many children took part in the survey?　　40 ✓

This line graph shows how many children attended swimming lessons each day during 1 week.

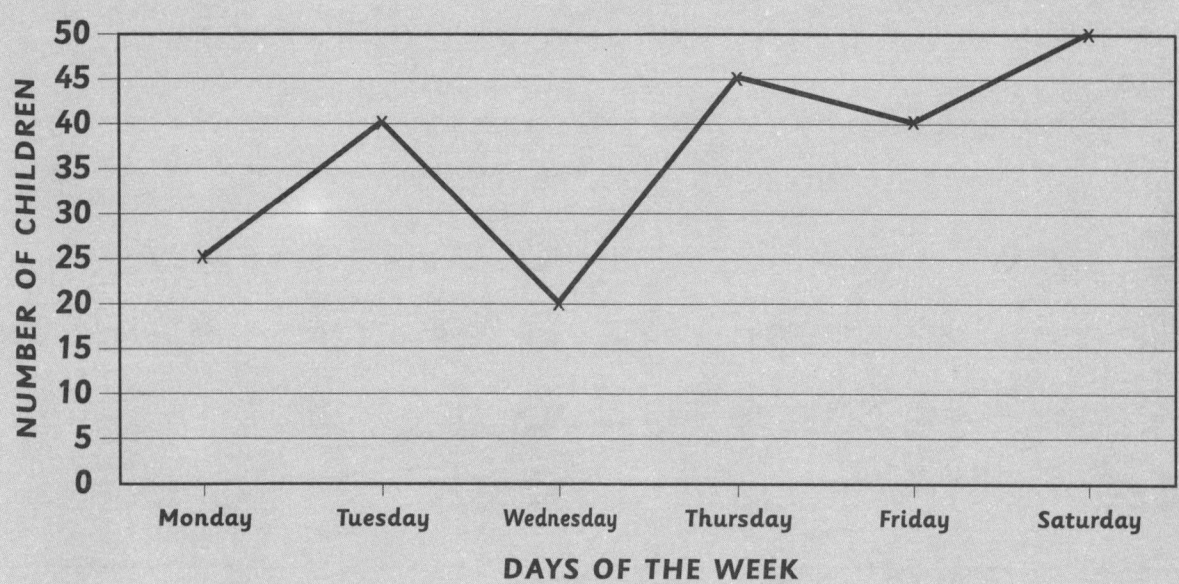

15　How many children attended on Thursday?　　45 ✓

16　On which 2 days was the attendance the same?　　Friday ✓
　　　　　　　　　　　　　　　　　　　　　　　　tuesday ✓

17　Which day had the lowest attendance?　　Wednesday ✓

18　Which was the most popular day?　　Saturday ✓

19　How many children attended in total on Wednesday, Thursday and Friday?　　105 ✓

9

Number/Shape, Space and Measures/ Handling Data

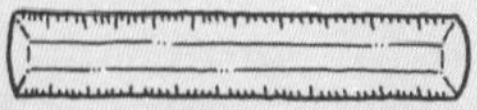

TEST 4

You will need: a ruler

Write these numbers in descending order (highest first).

1 124   142   241   421   214   412

421 ✓ 412 ✓ 241 ✓ 214 ✓ 142 ✓ 124 ✓

Write +, −, x or ÷ in each circle to make the calculation correct.

2 (4 + 6) ◯× 3 = 30 ✓

3 (7 x 8) ◯− 6 = 50 ✓

4 (19 ◯− 8) x 5 = 55 ✓

5 (60 ÷ 12) ◯× 7 = 35 ✓

6 (40 ◯÷ 4) + 19 = 29 ✓

7 (15 ◯+ 30) ÷ 9 = 5 ✓

8 (6 ◯× 7) + 23 = 65 ✓

9 (25 ◯− ◯− 45) ÷ 10 = 7 ✓

Use your ruler to measure the perimeter of this rectangle.

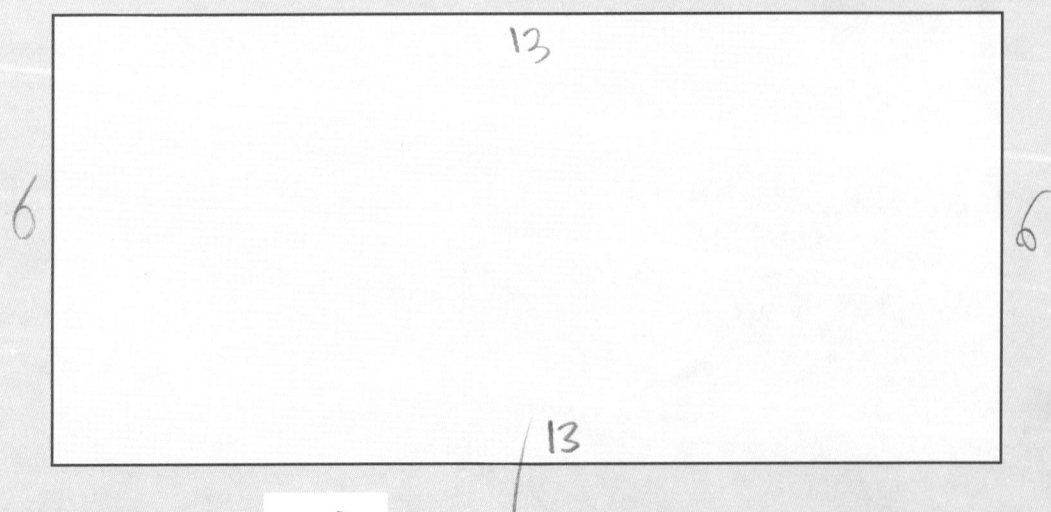

10 Perimeter = 38 cm ✓

NUMBER/SHAPE, SPACE AND MEASURES/HANDLING DATA   TEST 4

This machine multiplies numbers by 2 and then adds 7. Write the answers.

11. 6 → 19
12. 8 → 23
13. 10 → 27
14. 5 → 17
15. 12 → 31

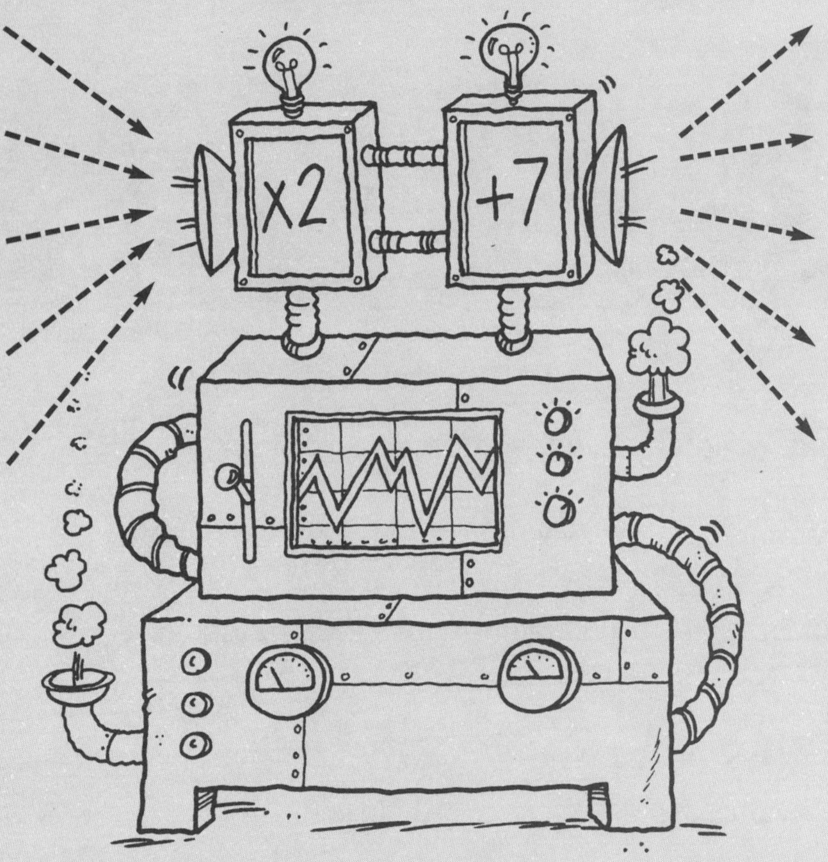

16. Turn Shape **A** clockwise through 1 right angle. Draw its new position.

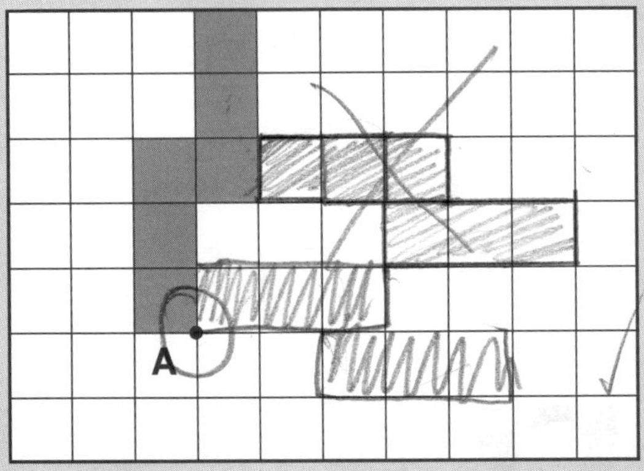

17. Draw a shape with an area larger than that of Shape **B**.

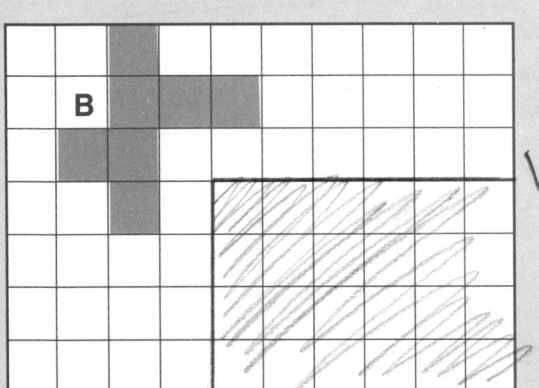

TEST 4   NUMBER/SHAPE, SPACE AND MEASURES/HANDLING DATA

This block graph shows how many children in a class have their birthdays in each month of the year.

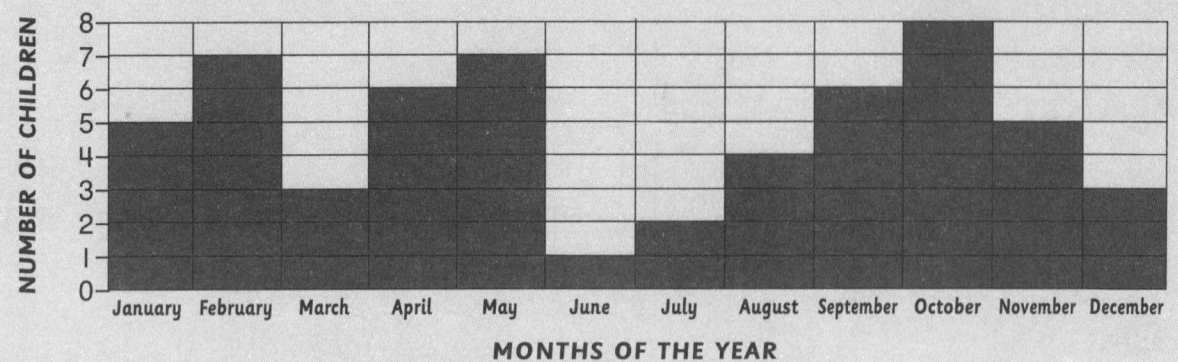

18 How many children have their birthdays in May?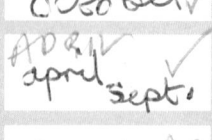

19 In which month do the most children have their birthdays?

20 In which 2 months do 6 children have their birthdays?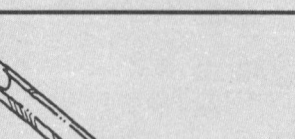

21 How many children are there in the class? 57 ✓

rubber 10p   postcard 15p   pencil 16p

22 How much would you have to pay for 2 postcards and 1 rubber? 40 ✓ p

23 How much would you have to pay for 1 rubber and 1 postcard? 25 p

24 How much would you have to pay for 2 pencils and 1 rubber? 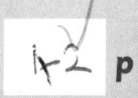 p

Number

TEST 5

You will need: a calculator

Write the missing numbers.

1) 3 [3] 7
   + 2 5 6
   ———
      5 9 3

2) 2 7 [5]
   ×   3
   ———
      8 2 5

3) 8 9 5
   − 2 [6] 3
   ———
      6 3 2

4) 5 3 8
   + 1 5 [6]
   ———
      6 9 4

5) 2 4 6
   ×   [3]
   ———
      7 3 8

Write the missing numbers.
There is more than one answer to each question.

6) [70] − [3] = 67

7) [100] + [5] = 105

8) 9 × [12] = 108

9) [11] × [8] = 88

10) 9 ÷ [1] = 9

11) [90] − [1] = 89

Treble the number and then subtract 2. Write the missing numbers.

12) 2 → 4 → 10 → [46]

13) 3 → 7 → 19 → [86]

14) 4 → 10 → 28 → [126]

Use all the number cards to make an addition sum. The answer must not be greater than 70.

5   3   2   8

15)
```
    2 8
+   3 5
   ———
    6 3
```

TEST 5   NUMBER

Look at these packs of stickers.

Flags of the world 14p   Footballers 16p

Pop stars 20p   Wild animals 12p

16 Sarah buys 1 pack of "Pop stars" and 1 pack of "Wild animals". How much does she spend?   32 ✓ p

17 How much will Ranjit pay for 1 pack of "Wild animals" and 2 packs of "Pop stars"?   52 ✓ p

18 Ben buys 2 packs of "Footballers" and pays with a 50p coin. How much change will he get?   18 ✓ p

19 Lucy buys 1 pack of "Flags of the world". She pays exactly the right amount with 5 coins. What are they?

| 5 p | 5 p | 2 p | 1 p | 1 ✓ p |

20 If I bought a pack of each of the sets of stickers, how much would they cost altogether?   62 ✓ p

NUMBER TEST 5

These items were all reduced by 50% in a sale. Write the new prices.

21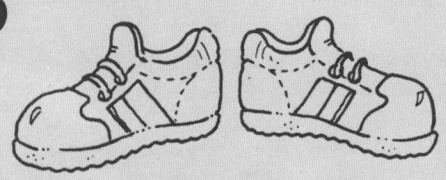
Shoes £26.48   £ 13.24 ✓

22
Shorts £8.80   £ 4.40 ✓

23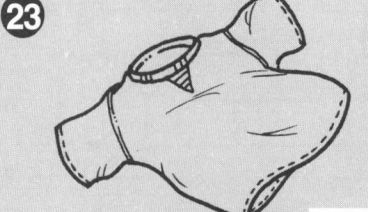
T-shirt £9.00   £ 4.50 ✓

24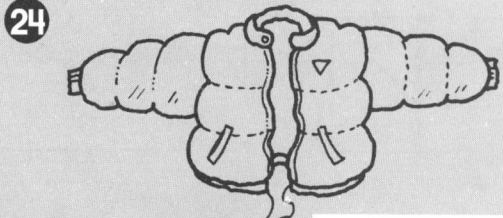
Jacket £32.00   £ 16.00 ✓

Write the largest number you can make with each set of 4 digits.

| 2 | 5 | 9 | 3 | | 5 | 2 | 8 | 6 | | 0 | 9 | 7 | 3 | | 3 | 2 | 1 | 5 |

25 9532 ✓   **26** 8652 ✓   **27** 9730 ✓   **28** 5321 ✓

Write the value of the letter in each of these sums.

29 $3n = 30$
n = 10 ✓

30 $b + 16 = 24$
b = 8 ✓

31 $c \div 5 = 100$
c = 20 ✗

32 $35 + d = 80$
d = 45 ✓

33 What is 2/3 of 60?   40 ✓
34 What is 3/5 of 100?   60 ✓

35 What is 25% of 80?   20 ✓
36 What is 1/3 of 90?   30 ✓

37 Write 0.25 as a fraction. $\frac{1}{4}$ ✓
38 Write 0.75 as a percentage.   75% ✓

15

Shape, Space and Measures

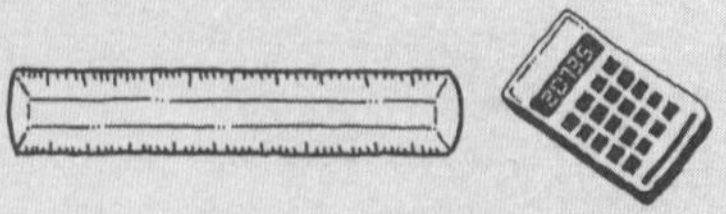

TEST 6

You will need: a ruler, a calculator

Complete these symmetrical shapes.

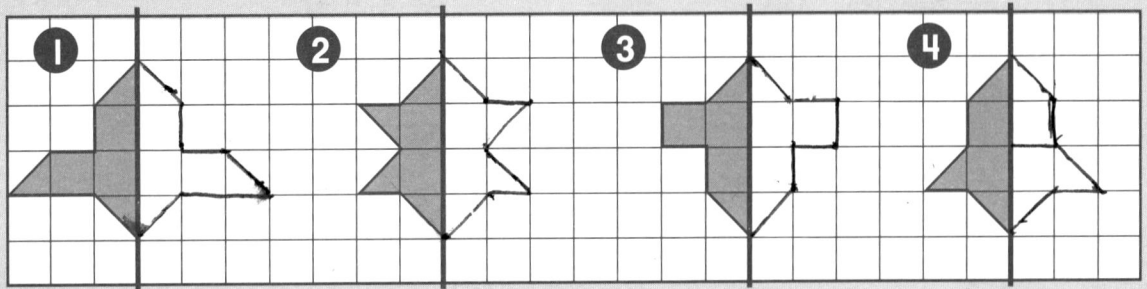

5. Draw a quadrilateral on the grid. It must have only one pair of parallel sides and these must be unequal in length.

What is the name of the quadrilateral?

Trapezium ✓

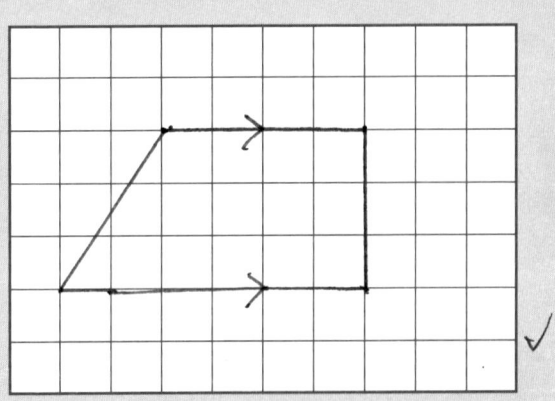 ✓

Put a cross ✗ under each acute angle and a tick ✓ under each obtuse angle.

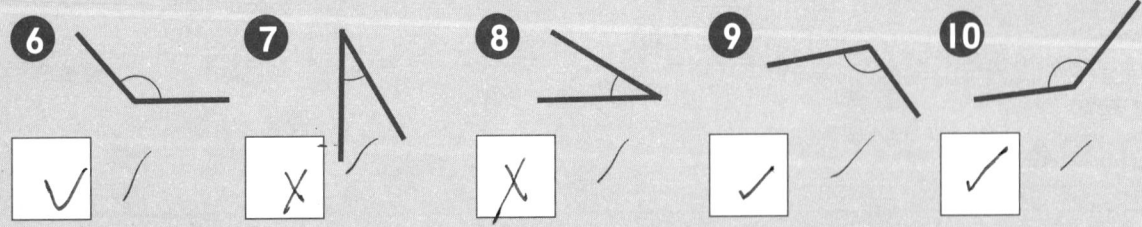

6. ✓ /
7. ✗
8. ✗ /
9. ✓
10. ✓

What is the area of this rectangle?

What is its perimeter?

40 cm
35 cm

11. Area = 1,400 cm² /

12. Perimeter = 150 cm /

16

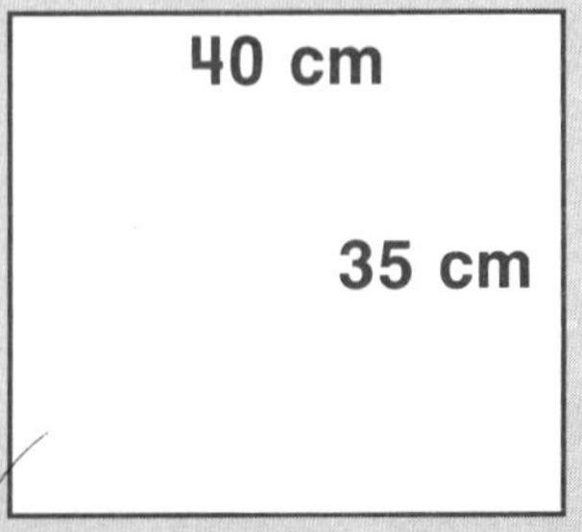

SHAPE, SPACE AND MEASURES   TEST 6

Use your ruler to find the area of this triangle.

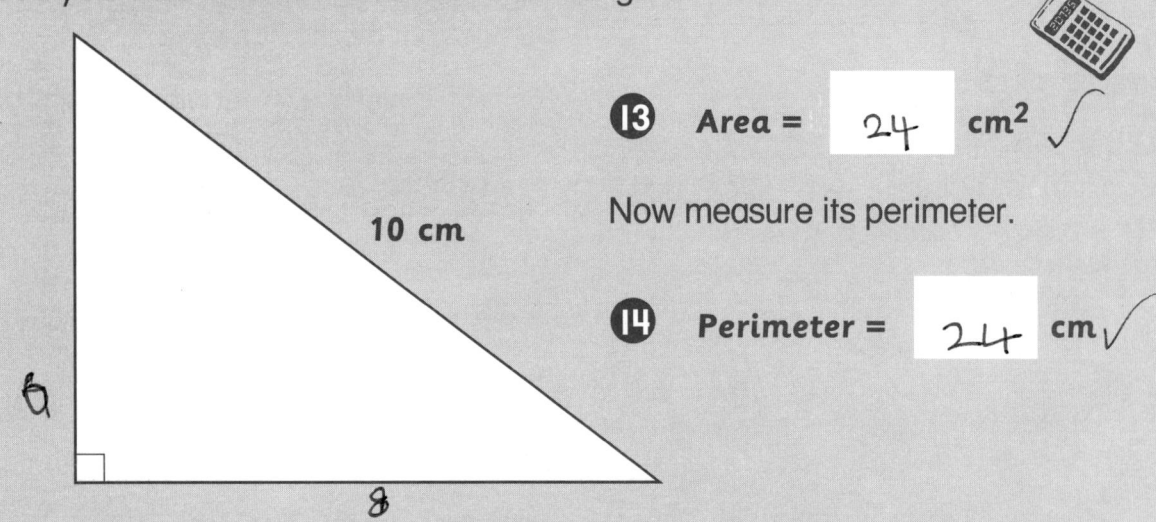

⑬ Area = 24 cm² ✓

Now measure its perimeter.

⑭ Perimeter = 24 cm ✓

Alice is covering her noticeboard with postcards which all measure 6 cm x 10 cm. The noticeboard measures 36 cm x 80 cm.

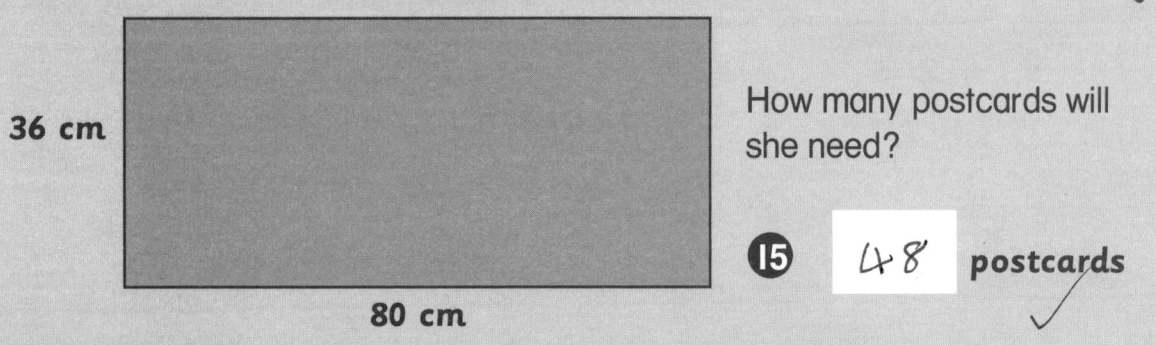

How many postcards will she need?

⑮ 48 postcards ✓

Points **A**, **B** and **C** are the three corners of a triangle.
What are the coordinates of:

⑯ Point **A**? 1,6 ✓

⑰ Point **B**? 6,4 ✓

⑱ Point **C**? 3,2 ✓

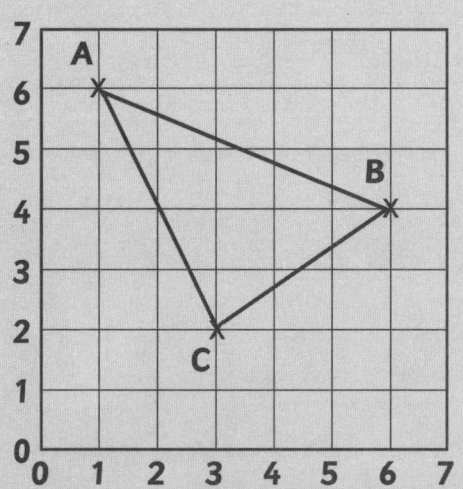

Handling Data

TEST 7

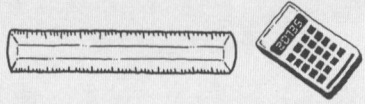

You will need: a ruler, a calculator

A group of children took part in a survey to find their favourite sweets. This pie chart shows the results.

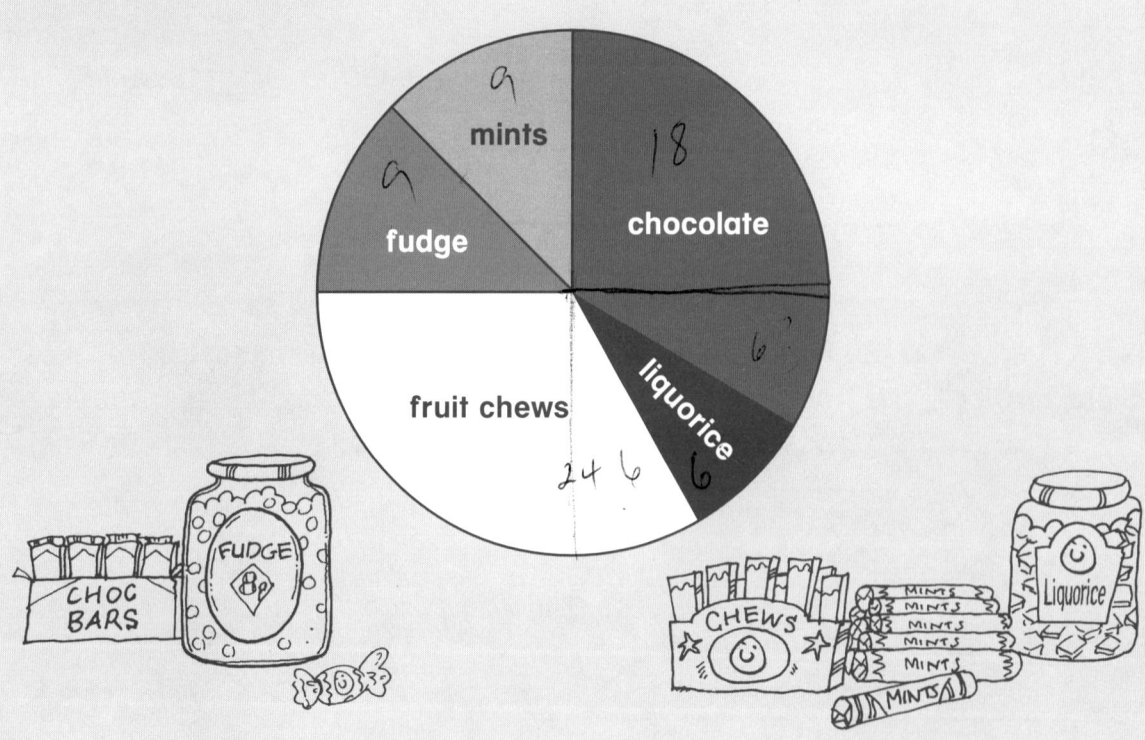

If 6 children chose liquorice and 24 chose fruit chews:

1. What percentage of the children chose mints?   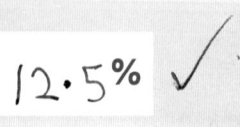 12.5% ✓

2. Estimate what fraction of the children chose liquorice. $\frac{1}{12}$ ✓

3. Estimate how many chose chocolate.   24 $\frac{1}{3}$ ✗

4. Estimate how many chose fudge.   9 $\frac{1}{7}$ ✗

5. How many children took part in the survey?   72 ✓

HANDLING DATA TEST 7

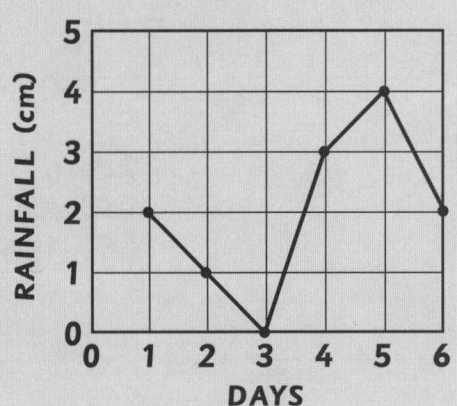

This line graph shows how much rain fell each day in a 6-day period.

6 How much rain fell on Day 4? **3 cm** ✓

7 On which day did no rain fall? **Day 3** ✓

8 On which day was the highest rainfall recorded? **Day 5** ✓

9 What was the average rainfall for the 6 days? **2 cm** ✓

10 How much rain fell in total during the week? **12 cm** ✓

Charles	5
Gemma	3
Prabu	6
Sita	4
Connor	3

This list shows how many merit stars a group of children were awarded.
If each star was worth 5 points, how many points did each child get?

11 Charles **25** ✓ **12** Gemma **15** ✓

13 Prabu **30** ✓ **14** Sita **20** ✓ **15** Connor **15** ✓

16 – 20 Draw a line graph to show this information. Complete the scale for the number of points.

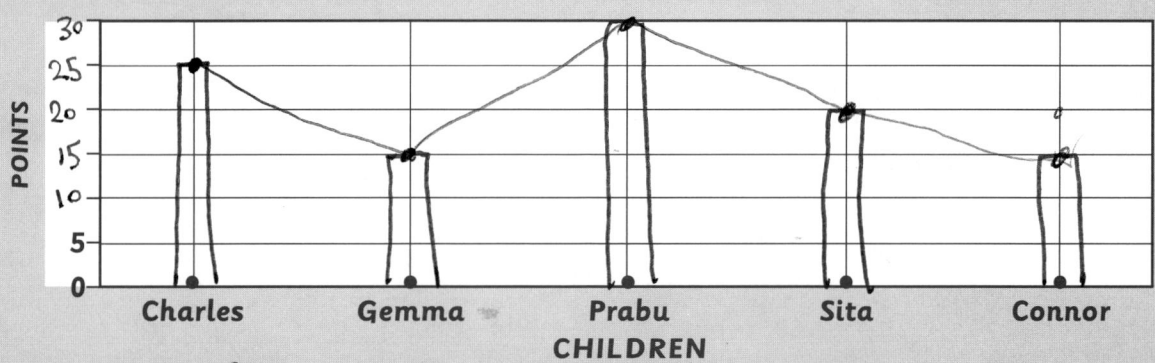

THIS IS NOT A LINE GRAPH

TEST 7 — HANDLING DATA

This chart shows how many magazines were sold in a local shop each day.

	Computers Weekly	Car Care	Nature	Outer Space
Monday	26	8	6	5
Tuesday	15	10	8	6
Wednesday	16	12	8	7
Thursday	10	9	5	3
Friday	8	10	7	5
Saturday	12	15	10	9
Sunday	0	0	0	0

21 Which magazine was the best seller for the week?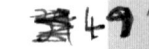

22 Which magazine had the lowest sales?

23 How many magazines were sold altogether on Tuesday?

24 On which day were the most magazines sold?

25 How many copies of "Nature" were sold altogether that week?

Number/Shape, Space and Measures/ Handling Data

TEST 8

You will need: a ruler, a calculator

Write the missing numbers.

1   1 [2] 4
      ─────────
      6) 7 4 4

2   1 5 9
      ─────────
      5) 7 [9] 5

3   1 0 3
      ─────────
      8) 8 2 [4]

4   8 3
      ─────────
      3) 2 [4] 9

This calculation has the same number missing from each box.

What is it? [8]

5   [8] × [8] − [8] = 56

The line from **A** to **B** divides the area of this grid into halves.

6 Divide the area of this grid into halves. Start at **A** and go along the lines to **B**.

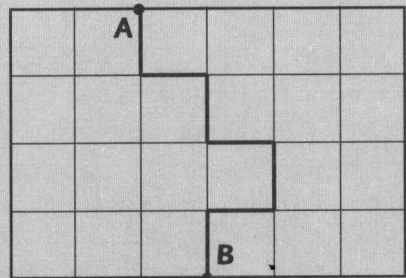

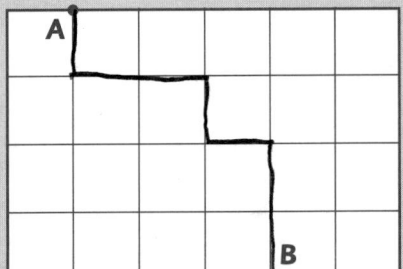

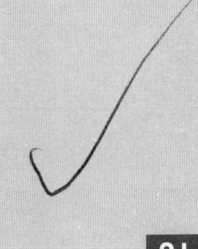

21

TEST 8   NUMBER/SHAPE, SPACE AND MEASURES/HANDLING DATA

This list gives the heights of 6 children.

Ben	160 cm	Alex	149 cm
Adam	125 cm	Gopal	150 cm
Hannah	129 cm	Rava	145 cm

7 – 9 Use this information to complete the bar chart.

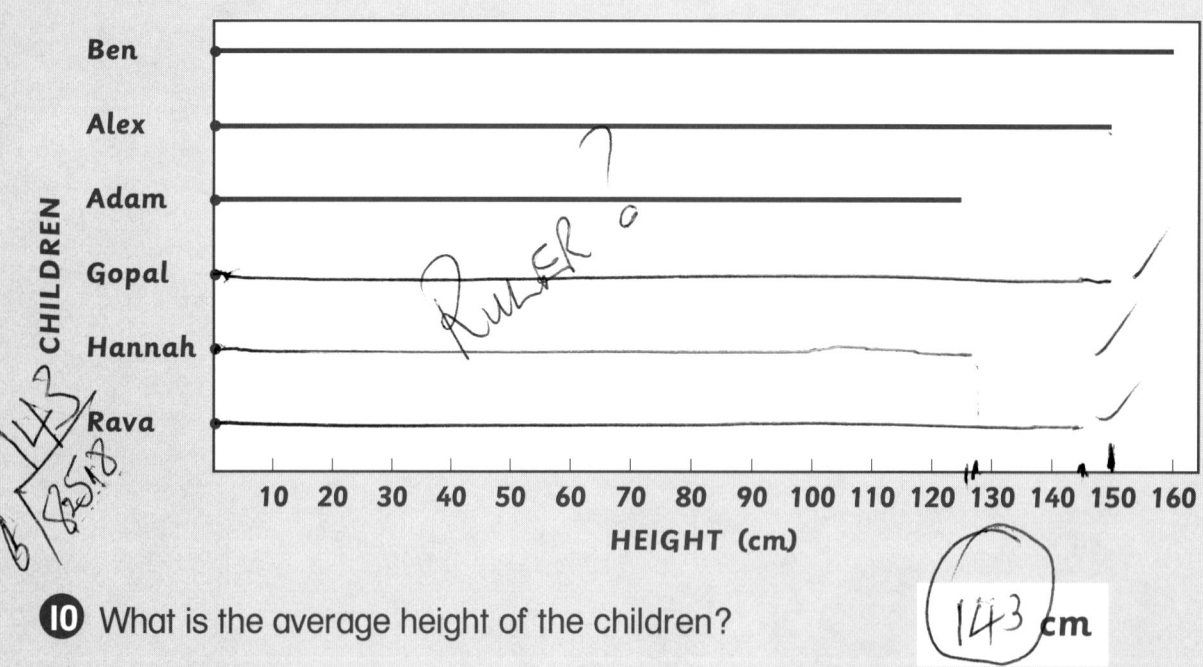

10 What is the average height of the children?   143 cm

Which shape can be folded to make a cube? Put a tick ✓ next to the shape.

11

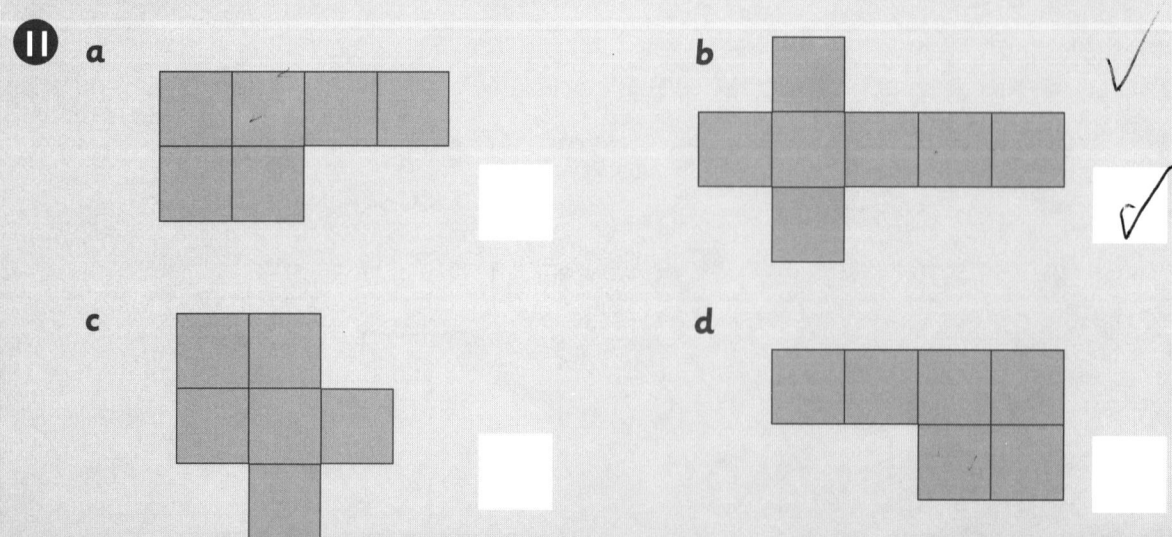

NUMBER/SHAPE, SPACE AND MEASURES/HANDLING DATA   TEST 8

What percentage of each flag is shaded?

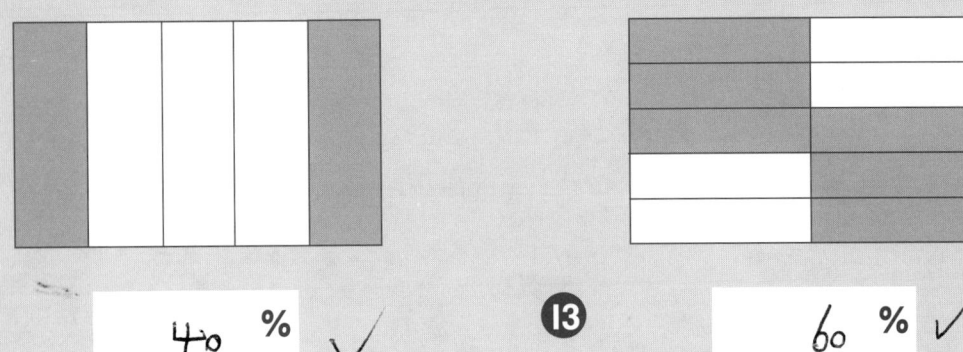

(12) 40 % ✓

(13) 60 % ✓

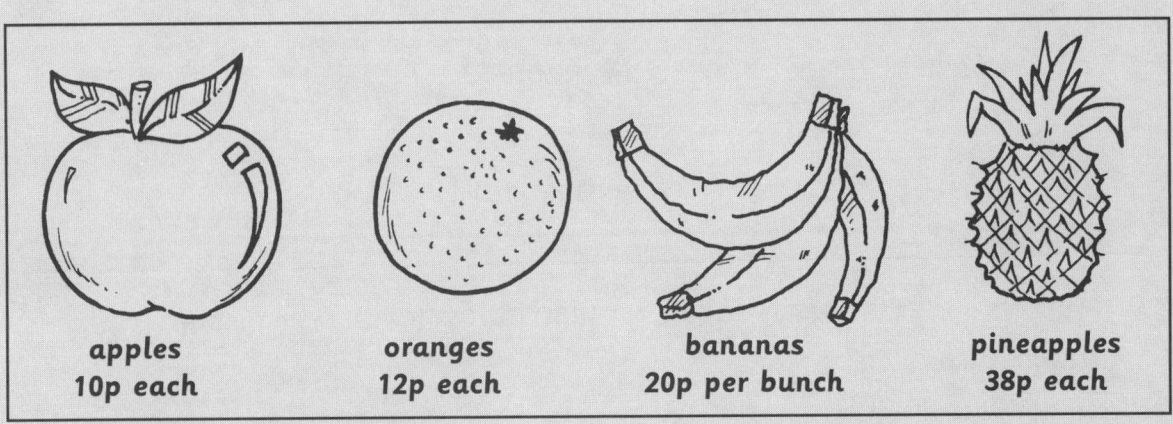

apples
10p each

oranges
12p each

bananas
20p per bunch

pineapples
38p each

(14) What is the cost of 10 apples and 4 oranges?   £1.48 ✓

(15) What is the cost of 1 pineapple and 8 apples?   £1.18 ✓

(16) What is the cost of 7 bunches of bananas?   £1.40 ✓

(17) – (18) What is the cost of 3 pineapples and 12 bunches of bananas?   £3.54 ✗

38×3 114
12×20 240
     3.54

How much change will I get from £5.00?   £1.480 ✗

(19) How many oranges could I buy for £1.80?   15 ✓

23

Number

TEST 9

You will need: a calculator

Write the missing numbers.

① 1 [4] 1   ② 1 5 6   ③ 1 2 4   ④ 2 9 9
  6)8 4 6   5)7 [8] 0   8)9 9 [2]   3)[8] 9 7

⑤ Pencils cost £1.63 per pack. How much do 100 packs cost?   £163.00

⑥ Books cost £5.76 per pack. How much do 10 packs cost?   £57.60

⑦ Paper costs 10p per sheet. How much do 580 sheets cost?   5800 p

Which is larger, **a)** 40% of 60 or **b)** ⁴/₅ of 40?

⑧ [B] is larger.   ⑨ The difference is [8].

On a school trip the teacher bought 8 lollipops at 26p each and 9 ice creams at 30p each.

⑩ How much did he have to pay?   £4.78

A group of children visit a museum. They are in groups of 18, and each group must be accompanied by an adult. If there are 12 adults, how many children are there?

⑪ [216] children

NUMBER   TEST 9

Write each of these fractions as a percentage.

(12) 1/4 = 25 %   (13) 1/2 = 50 %   (14) 3/4 = 75 %

(15) 3/5 = 60 %   (16) 3/10 = 30 %   (17) 1/3 = $33\frac{1}{3}$ %

(18) 6(2.36 + 5.62) = 47.88   (19) 4(8.79 + 2.79) = 46.32

(20) 5(3.19 + 8.26) = 57.25   (21) 3(6.43 + 2.87) = 27.9

Find the mean for each row.

(22)   3   8   12   9   8

(23)   75   25   50   150   75

(24)   8   7   13   14   6   11   4   9

(25)   26p 30p 8p   56p 50p   34p

A video cassette costs £8.00. If **n** is the number of cassettes bought and **t** is the total price paid, write the formula for finding the total price paid.

  £8.00 × n = T   ✗ T = £8.00 × n

Draw a ring round the number which is 1/100 of 5600.

(27)   5006   516   5060   (56)   650

Shape, Space and Measures

TEST 10

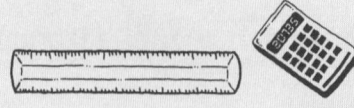

You will need: a ruler: a calculator

The scale on this map is 1 cm : 6 km. Use your ruler to find the distance between Smalltown and Penbury.

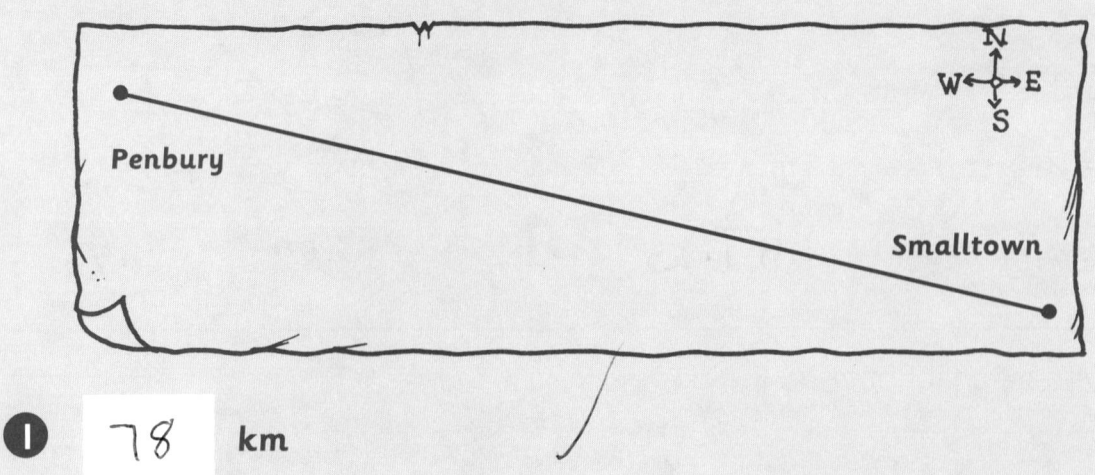

1 78 km

The area of this rectangle is 432 cm².

2 How long is it?

36 cm ✓

12 cm

A triangle has these properties:

- It has 3 equal sides.
- It has 3 equal angles.
- It has reflective symmetry.
- It does not contain any right angles.

3 What kind of triangle is it?   equilateral

SHAPE, SPACE AND MEASURES — TEST 10

Calculate the area and perimeter of each of these triangles.

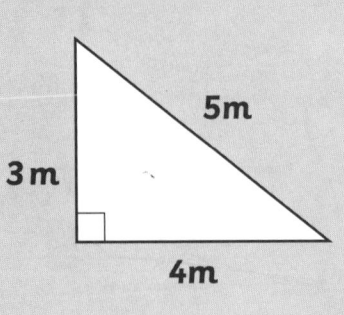
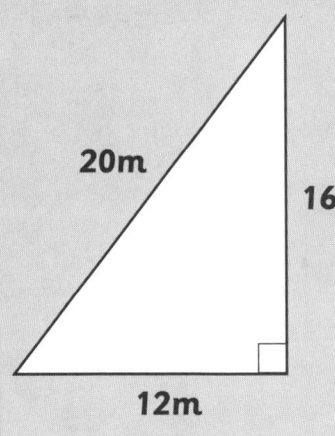
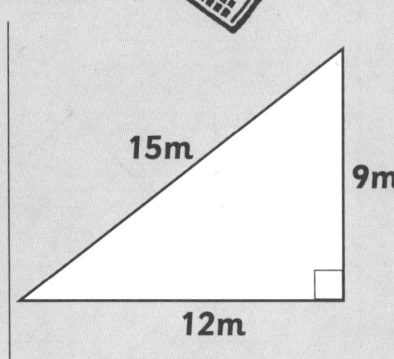

④ Area = ~~96~~ 6 m²   ⑥ Area = 96 m²   ⑧ Area = 54 m²

⑤ Perimeter = 12 m   ⑦ Perimeter = 48 m   ⑨ Perimeter = 36 m

Work out the volume of each box.

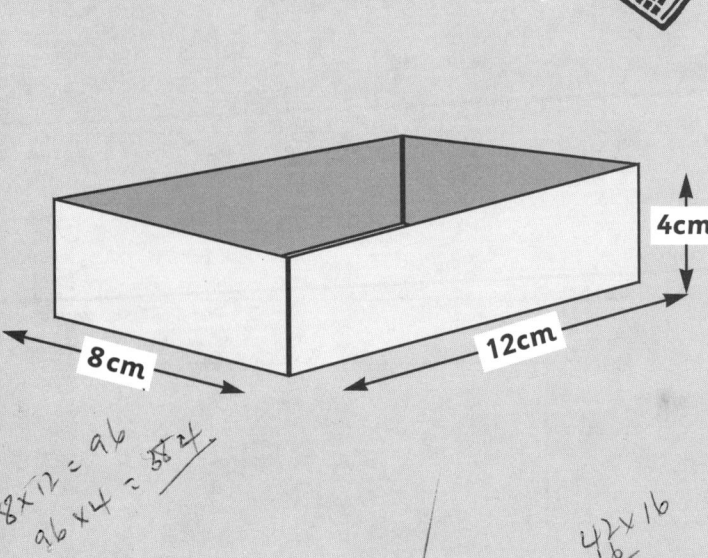
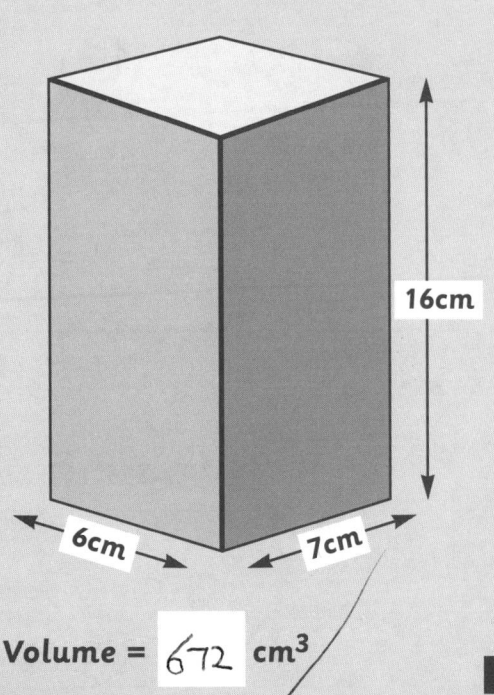

8×12 = 96
96×4 = 384

42×16
420
252
672

⑩ Volume = 384 cm³   ⑪ Volume = 672 cm³

27

TEST 10   SHAPE, SPACE AND MEASURES

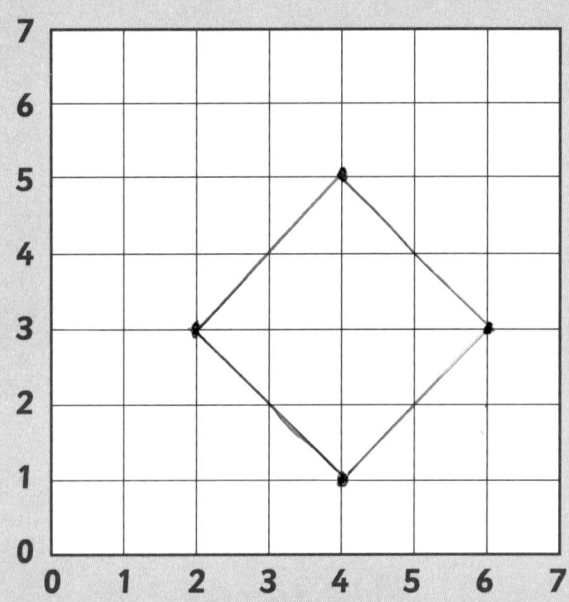

Draw a shape using these coordinates:

A (2, 3)
B (4, 5)
C (6, 3)
D (4, 1)

12 What shape have you drawn?

a Square ✓

This picture is twice as wide as it is high. Its perimeter is 252 cm.

13 What is the width of the picture?   121 ✗

14 What is the height of the picture?   12 ✗

This flag has an area of 650cm². The shaded part covers 30% of the flag.

15 What is the area of the shaded part?   5.6 cm² ✗

28

Handling Data

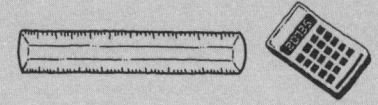

TEST 11

You will need: a ruler, a calculator

1 – 6 Draw a line graph to show this information.

Number of children	6	3	2	5	4	1	0
Favourite flower	rose	lily	iris	daffodil	poppy	tulip	crocus

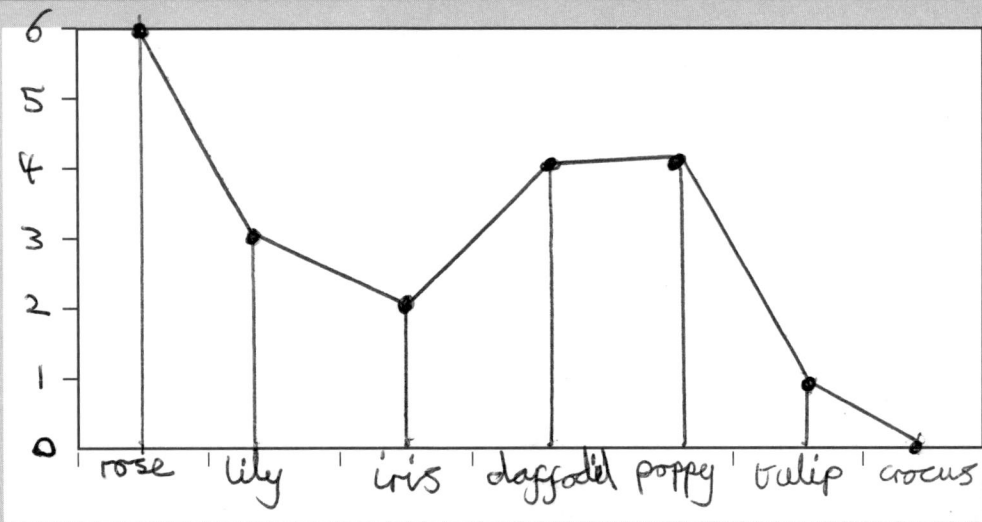

This table shows the average temperatures in different countries on the same day.

Sweden	5°C
Britain	13°C
Portugal	19°C
Greenland	−25°C
Russia	−5°C

Put the place names and temperatures in order, starting with the warmest.

7	Portugal	19°C
8	Britain	13°C
9	Sweden	5°C
10	~~Greenland~~ Russia	−5°C
11	Greenland	−25°C

TEST 11   HANDLING DATA

This pie chart shows how many cakes a bakery sold one day.

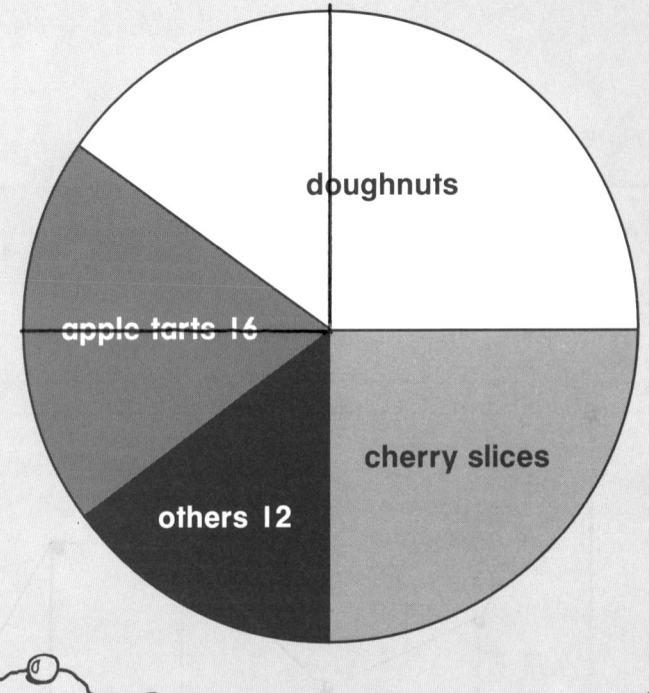

80 cakes were sold altogether.

12 If 1/4 of these were cherry slices, how many cherry slices were sold?   20

13 What percentage of all the cakes sold were doughnuts?   40

14 What fraction of all the cakes sold were apple tarts?   1/5

15 What percentage of all the cakes sold were not apple tarts?   80

HANDLING DATA TEST 11

This block graph shows how many Watersplash washing machines were sold in a 6-month period.

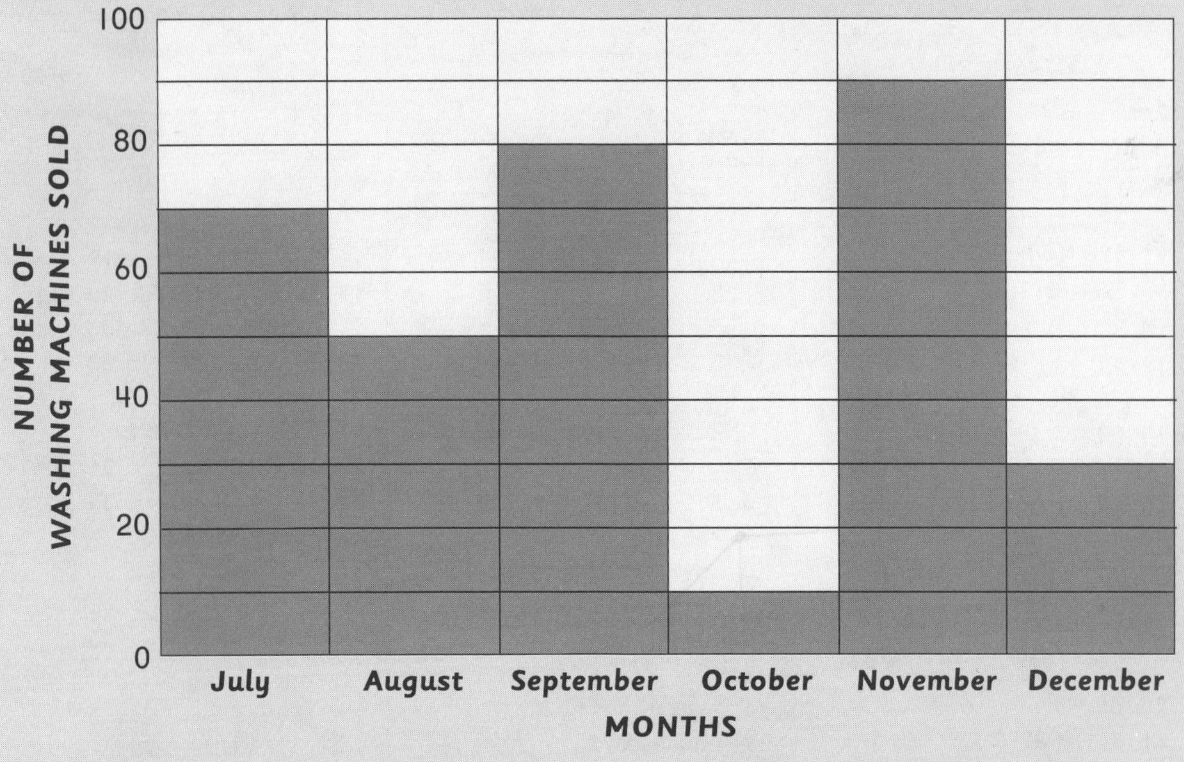

Use the block graph to complete this table which shows the trend in sales from month to month.

July–August	down 20
August–September	up 30
16 September–October	down 70
17 October–November	up 80
November–December	down 60

18 Which month had the highest sales?   November

19 What were the average sales over the 6 months?   55

31

ANSWERS

TEST 1
1
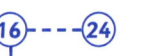

2 ×   3 ÷   4 ×
5 +   6 ×   7 ÷
8 ÷   9 +   10 −

11 120 |150| 205 276 |301|
    304 |310| |323|

12–14

15 23 17 (49) 38 24 (48)

16–19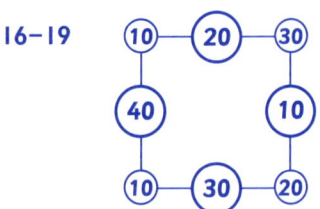

20 88
21 4   22 7   23 4
24 6
25 |6| 3   26 |30| |35|
27 |32| |64| 28 |243| |27|
29 |100| |125|

TEST 2
1 Each shape contains at least 1 right angle.
2 Each shape has straight edges.
3 13cm
4–8
9 ✓   10 ✗
11 ✓   12 ✗
13 34m   14 10 squares
15 By counting the squares on the grid
16 Accept any shape which covers 10 squares

17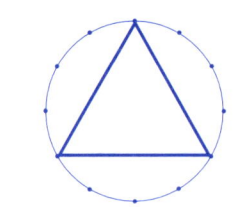

TEST 3
1–4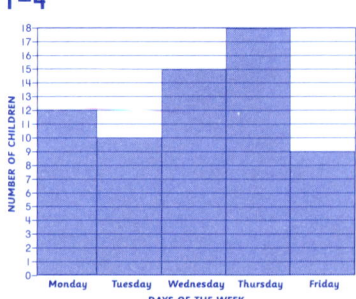

5 15   6 25   7 5
8 95   9 coaches
10 Grange Hill   11 10
12 15   13 Newsround
14 40
15 45
16 Tuesday and Friday
17 Wednesday
18 Saturday   19 105

TEST 4
1 421 412 241 214 142 124
2 ×   3 −   4 −
5 ×   6 ÷   7 +
8 ×   9 +
10 38cm   11 19   12 23
13 27   14 17   15 31
16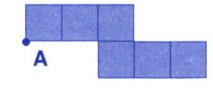
17 Accept any shape with an area of more than 7 squares.
18 7   19 October
20 April and September
21 57
22 40p   23 25p   24 42p

TEST 5
1 3   2 5   3 6
4 6   5 3
6–11 Accept any numbers which make the equations correct.
12 28   13 55   14 82
15   28   38
      +35   or   +25
       63   63

16 32p   17 52p   18 18p
19 5p 5p 2p 1p 1p   20 62p
21 £13.24   22 £4.40
23 £4.50   24 £16.00
25 9532   26 8652
27 9730   28 5321
29 10   30 8   31 500
32 45   33 40   34 60
35 20   36 30
37 1/4   38 75%

TEST 6
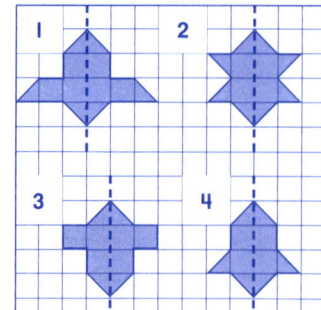

5 a trapezium
6 ✓   7 ✗   8 ✗
9 ✓   10 ✓
11 1400cm²   12 150cm
13 24cm²   14 24cm
15 48 postcards
16 (1, 6)   17 (6, 4)   18 (3, 2)

TEST 7
1. 12½% 2. 1/12 3. 24
4. 9 5. 72
6. 3cm
7. Day 3 8. Day 5 9. 2cm
10. 12cm
11. 25 12. 15
13. 30 14. 20 15. 15
16–20

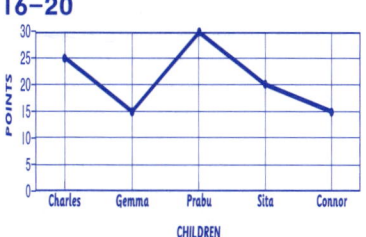

21. Computers Weekly
22. Outer Space
23. 39 24. Saturday
25. 44

TEST 8
1. 2 2. 9 3. 4
4. 4
5. 8
6. Accept any line from **A** to **B** as long as there is the same number of squares on each side of the line.

7–9

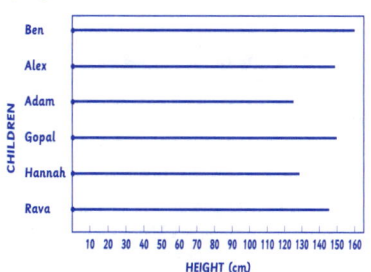

10. 143cm
11. b ✓
12. 40% 13. 60%
14. £1.48 15. £1.18
16. £1.40 17. £3.54
18. £1.46 19. 15 oranges

TEST 9
1. 4 2. 8 3. 2
4. 8 5. £163
6. £57.60 7. £58
8. b 9. 8
10. £4.78 11. 216
12. 25% 13. 50%
14. 75% 15. 60%
16. 30% 17. 33⅓%
18. 47.88 19. 46.32
20. 57.25 21. 27.9
22. 8 23. 75
24. 9 25. 34p
26. t = £8 × n 27. 56

TEST 10
1. 78km 2. 36cm
3. an equilateral triangle
4. 6m² 5. 12m 6. 96m²
7. 48m 8. 54m² 9. 36m
10. 384cm³ 11. 672cm³
12. a square

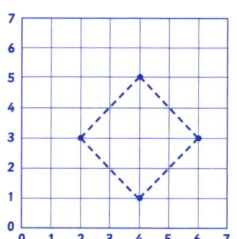

13. 84cm 14. 42cm
15. 195cm²

TEST 11
1–6

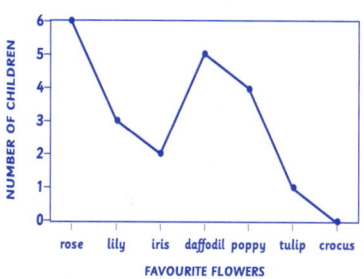

7. Portugal   19°C
8. Britain   13°C
9. Sweden   5°C
10. Russia   −5°C
11. Greenland −25°C
12. 20 13. 40%
14. 1/5 15. 80%
16. down 70 17. up 80
18. November
19. 55

Text © Jim Fitzsimmons and Rhona Whiteford 1997

Illustrations © Sascha Lipscomb 1997

The right of Jim Fitzsimmons and Rhona Whiteford to be identified as the authors of this work have been asserted by them in accordance with the Copyright, Design and Patents Act 1988.

First published in Great Britain 1997

All rights reserved. No part of this publication may be reproduced, stored in a retrieval system, or transmitted, in any form or by any means, without the prior written permission of the publisher, nor be otherwise circulated in any form of binding or cover other than that in which it is published and without a similar condition being imposed on the subsequent purchaser.

Published by
Hodder Children's Books,
a division of Hodder Headline plc,
338 Euston Road, London NW1 3BH

Printed and bound in Great Britain

A CIP record is registered by and held at the British Library.

The National Curriculum for English is divided into three parts: **Speaking and listening**, **Reading**, and **Writing**. This chart lists the tests you will find in this book together with a range of marks that will help you to make a more informed assessment of your child's level of performance. The skills are also outlined so that you can give support in areas where help is needed. The SATs are assessed by a trained marker, but your test results are valuable as a guide.

These tests are just like the SATs, but remember that tests do not measure everything that children do; the teacher will also make an assessment of performance over the whole year. This is particularly important for **Speaking and listening**, which is not covered in the written tests.

READING
Reading and comprehension skills
Reading aloud expressively, fluently and with confidence, understanding fiction and non-fiction texts, using deduction, inference and previous reading experience, developing preferences and views and supporting them by reference to details in a text, distinguishing between fact and opinion, becoming aware of style

Reading and comprehension assessment

Test	Marks	Total	C	B	A
1	34	44	5-10	11-34	35-44
2	10				
3	11	36	5-10	11-25	26-36
4	12				
5	13				

WRITING
Story writing skills
Writing independently using correct punctuation and grammar and a clear, legible style, writing stories that have a beginning, a middle and an ending, writing chronological non-fiction such as a factual report or letter, writing for different purposes and audiences (a list, an instruction, a greeting, a warning), expressing feelings and emotions, planning, revising and drafting

Story writing assessment

In the following four tests the performance should be assessed by the marker.

6 Base your assessment on the story structure and the amount of detail. **10 marks total**
7 Base your assessment on the use of the plan, the story structure, the use of correct grammar and punctuation, the handwriting, the vocabulary and the style. **10 marks total**
8 Base your assessment on the clarity of the main message. **10 marks total**
9 Base your assessment on the use of the plan, the use of correct grammar and punctuation, the handwriting and the style. **10 marks total**

Test	Marks	Total	C	B	A
6-9		40	5-10	11-29	30-40

Spelling skills
Spelling correctly in their own writing, checking spelling, using common letter strings (**tion**, **ing**) and word families (**look**, **looked**, **looking**, **looks**), using prefixes (**bi**cycle, **dis**believe) and suffixes (walk**ing**, happ**ily**), using apostrophes for contractions (**can't**)

Spelling assessment

Test	Marks	Total	C	B	A
10	55	55	5-15	16-29	30-55

Handwriting skills
Producing fluent, legible joined-up writing with well-defined ascenders (**lhk**), descenders (**gpy**) and capitals, using different forms of handwriting for different purposes: fast writing for notes, neat print for labels, smooth, neat joined-up writing for a finished narrative

Handwriting assessment

Performance should be assessed by the marker.

Test	Marks	Total	C	B	A
11	20	20	5-8	9-14	15-20

Key
C Your child has an average understanding of this area. Regular practice at home using workbooks will build their skills and confidence.
B Your child has a good understanding of this area, but further practice will improve their performance.
A Your child has a very good grasp of this area. Continued practice will help them achieve the best possible results.

HODDER HOME LEARNING

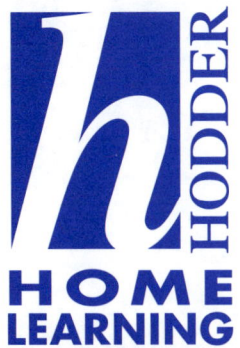

SATs Practice in English

AGE 11

Rhona Whiteford and Jim Fitzsimmons

Illustrated by John Eastwood

The National Curriculum for England and Wales requires all 11 year-olds to be tested in the subjects of English, Mathematics and Science. These tests are called SATs (Standard Assessment Tasks), and are completed during the normal school day. Their purpose is to give schools information about what children are achieving compared to others of the same age, and to highlight areas where help is needed. This book will help you to prepare your child for the SATs in English. Although the SATs are taken at age 11, this book may be used for practice throughout Year 6.

How to help your child

a Working together

If you work through each test with your child, you may discover areas where extra practice is needed. You can provide this by choosing some interesting books and poems, and basing further questions on these.

b Test conditions

The SATs tests are timed at this stage, so you can use this book to prepare your child for real test conditions. Encourage them to work independently, with good concentration and as quickly as possible. Use the following times as a guide:

Reading

reading through – 15 minutes
writing answers – 45 minutes

Do Tests 1 and 2 as a block, then Tests 3, 4 and 5 together. Or, use each test individually with no time limit.

Writing story or letter

planning – 15 minutes
writing – 45 minutes

Handwriting

10 minutes

- Keep sessions short and frequent, perhaps one test per day.
- Make sure you and your child are relaxed and have a quiet place in which to work.
- Avoid putting your child under pressure.
- Build your child's confidence by offering plenty of praise and encouragement.

Hodder Children's Books

NATIONAL CONFEDERATION OF PARENT TEACHER ASSOCIATIONS

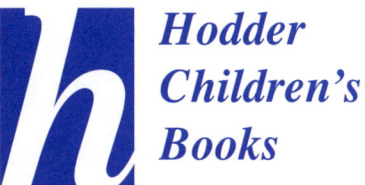

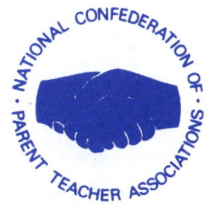

The only home learning programme supported by the NCPTA

Reading
COMPREHENSION: FICTION

TEST 1

This extract is from a book called *The Lion, the Witch and the Wardrobe* by C. S. Lewis. A boy called Edmund has gone out into the snows of the magic land of Narnia in search of the White Witch's House. He has already met her and is half under her spell, although he has been warned about her power by the kindly Beavers. He leaves his brother and two sisters and goes out alone.

> So he turned up his collar and shuffled across the top of the dam (luckily it wasn't so slippery since the snow had fallen) to the far side of the river.

> It was pretty bad when he reached the far side. It was growing darker every minute and what with that and the snowflakes swirling all round him he could hardly see three feet ahead. And then too there was no road. He kept slipping into deep drifts of snow, and skidding on frozen puddles, and tripping over fallen tree-trunks, and sliding down steep banks, and barking his shins against rocks, till he was wet and cold and bruised all over. The silence and the loneliness were dreadful. In fact I really think he might have given up the whole plan and gone back and owned up and made friends with the others, if he hadn't happened to say to himself, "When I'm King of Narnia the first thing I shall do will be to make some decent roads." And of course that set him off thinking about being a

COMPREHENSION: FICTION   TEST 1

King and all the other things he would do and this cheered him up a good deal.

He would never have found his way if the moon hadn't come out by the time he got to the other river. Even as it was, he got wet through for he had to stoop under branches and great loads of snow came sliding off on to his back. And every time this happened he thought more and more how he hated Peter — just as if all this had been Peter's fault.

But at last he came to a part where it was more level and the valley opened out. And there, on the other side of the river, quite close to him, in the middle of a little plain between two hills, he saw what must be the White Witch's House. And the moon was shining brighter than ever. The House was really a small castle. It seemed to be all towers; little towers with long pointed spires on them, sharp as needles. They looked like huge dunce's caps or sorcerer's caps. And they shone in the moonlight and their long shadows looked strange on the snow. Edmund began to be afraid of the House.

But it was too late to think about turning back now. He crossed the river on the ice and walked up to the House. There was nothing stirring; not the slightest sound anywhere. Even his own feet made no noise on the deep newly fallen snow. He walked on and on, past corner after corner of the House, and past turret after turret to find the door. He had to go right round to the far side before he found it. It was a huge arch but the great iron gates stood wide open.

Edmund crept up to the arch and looked inside into the courtyard, and there he saw a sight that nearly made his heart stop beating. Just inside the gate, with the moonlight shining on it, stood an enormous lion crouched as if it was ready to spring. And Edmund stood in the shadow of the arch, afraid to go on and afraid to go back, with his knees knocking together.

Then at last he began to wonder why the lion was standing so still — for it hadn't moved one inch since he first set eyes on it. Edmund remembered what the others had said about the White Witch turning people into stone. Perhaps this was only a stone lion. And as soon as he had thought of that he noticed that the lion's back and the top of its head were covered with snow. Of

TEST 1　　COMPREHENSION: FICTION

course it must be only a statue! No living animal would have let itself get covered with snow. Then very slowly and with his heart beating as if it would burst, Edmund ventured to go up to the lion. Even now he hardly dared to touch it, but at last he put out his hand, very quickly, and did. It was cold stone. He had been frightened of a mere statue!

The relief which Edmund felt was so great that in spite of the cold he suddenly got warm all over right down to his toes, and at the same time there came into his head what seemed a perfectly lovely idea. "Probably," he thought, "this is the great Lion Aslan that they were all talking about. She's caught him already and turned him into stone. So *that's* the end of all their fine ideas about him! Pooh! Who's afraid of Aslan?"

And he stood there gloating over the stone lion, and presently he did something very silly and childish. He took a stump of lead pencil out of his pocket and scribbled a moustache on the lion's upper lip and then a pair of spectacles on its eyes. Then he said, "Yah! Silly old Aslan! How do you like being a stone? You thought yourself mighty fine, didn't you?" But in spite of the scribbles on it the face of the great stone beast still looked so terrible, and sad, and noble, staring up in the moonlight, that Edmund didn't really get any fun out of jeering at it. He turned away and began to cross the courtyard.

As he got into the middle of it he saw that there were dozens of statues all about – standing here and there rather as the pieces stand on a chessboard when it is half-way through the game. There were stone satyrs, and stone wolves,

COMPREHENSION: FICTION   TEST 1

and bears and foxes and cat-a-mountains of stone. There were lovely stone shapes that looked like women but who were really the spirits of trees. There was the great shape of a centaur and a winged horse and a long lithe creature that Edmund took to be a dragon. They all looked so strange standing there perfectly life-like and also perfectly still, in the bright cold moonlight, that it was eerie work crossing the courtyard.

He now saw that there was a dim light showing from a doorway on the far side of the courtyard. He went to it, there was a flight of stone steps going up to an open door. Edmund went up them. Across the threshold lay a great wolf.

"It's all right, it's all right," he kept saying to himself; "it's only a stone wolf. It can't hurt me," and he raised his leg to step over it. Instantly the huge creature rose, with all the hair bristling along its back, opened a great, red mouth and said in a growling voice:

"Who's there? Who's there? Stand still, stranger, and tell me who you are."

"If you please, sir," said Edmund, trembling so that he could hardly speak, "my name is Edmund, and I'm the Son of Adam that Her Majesty met in the wood the other day and I've come to bring her the news that my brother and sisters are now in Narnia – quite close, in the Beavers' house. She – she wanted to see them."

"I will tell Her Majesty," said the Wolf. "Meanwhile, stand still on the threshold, as you value your life." Then it vanished into the house.

Edmund stood and waited, his fingers aching with cold and his heart pounding in his chest, and presently the grey wolf, Maugrim, the Chief of the Witch's Secret Police, came bounding back and said, "Come in! Come in! Fortunate favourite of the Queen – or else not so fortunate."

5

TEST 1 COMPREHENSION: FICTION

And Edmund went in, taking great care not to tread on the Wolf's paws.

He found himself in a long gloomy hall with many pillars, full, as the courtyard had been, of statues. The one nearest the door was a little faun with a very sad expression on its face, and Edmund couldn't help wondering if this might be Lucy's friend. The only light came from a single lamp and close beside this sat the White Witch.

"I'm come, your Majesty," said Edmund, rushing eagerly forward.

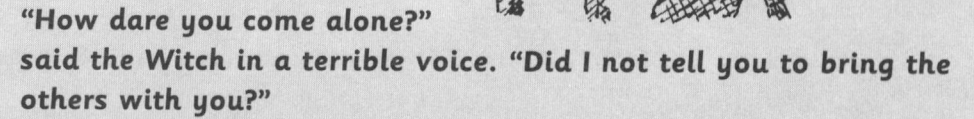

"How dare you come alone?" said the Witch in a terrible voice. "Did I not tell you to bring the others with you?"

"Please, your Majesty," said Edmund, "I've done the best I can. I've brought them quite close. They're in the little house on top of the dam just up the river — with Mr. and Mrs. Beaver."

A slow cruel smile came over the Witch's face.

"Is this all your news?" she asked.

"No, your Majesty," said Edmund, and proceeded to tell her all he had heard before leaving the Beavers' house.

"What! Aslan?" cried the Queen, "Aslan! Is this true? If I find you have lied to me —"

"Please, I'm only repeating what they said," stammered Edmund.

But the Queen, who was no longer attending to him, clapped her hands. Instantly the same dwarf whom Edmund had seen with her before appeared.

"Make ready our sledge," ordered the Witch, "and use the harness without bells."

Abridged from The Lion, the Witch and the Wardrobe *by C. S. Lewis*

COMPREHENSION: FICTION   TEST 1

■ QUESTIONS ■

The story

1. What was the weather like?

   raining ☐   dark and snowy ☐   light and warm ☐

2. Edmund was

   looking through a window ☐   on a journey ☐   in a cave ☐

3. What was shining on the snow?

   the sun ☐   a full moon ☐   a light ☐

4. When he found the White Witch's House, Edmund saw that it was really

   a big building ☐   a small castle ☐   white with snow ☐

5. What did Edmund see just inside the open gates of the huge arch?
   _____

6. When he saw that all the figures were made of stone, who did he think the stone lion was?

   the Witch herself ☐   no one special ☐   Aslan ☐

7. When Edmund crossed the courtyard he saw a great wolf lying across the threshold of the open door. Why did he get a shock when he tried to pass it?
   _____
   _____

8. Who did he meet next? _____

9. What news did Edmund tell the White Witch?

   all he had heard before leaving the Beavers' house ☐

   all about Aslan's plans ☐   all about his own plans ☐

TEST 1 COMPREHENSION: FICTION

■ **QUESTIONS** ■

The characters

10 Edmund thought he was very important and would soon be made even more important. What did he say he would become?

_____

11 What did Edmund do to the statue of the lion, and why?

_____
_____

12 – 14 Describe three things that were frightening about the wolf.

_____
_____
_____

15 – 16 Which two words might describe the Witch?

_____

_____

COMPREHENSION: FICTION   TEST 1

■ QUESTIONS ■

The style

17 – 18 The writer describes in detail two things that make Edmund's journey to the Witch's House so hard. What are they?

_____

_____

19 – 21 The writer takes Edmund to three different places. In one he is quite bold, in the second he is frightened and in the third he is shocked because he doesn't find what he expects. What are these places?

_____

_____

_____

22 – 24 Which three adjectives (describing words) does the writer use most often to describe the statues?

_____

_____

_____

9

TEST I   COMPREHENSION: FICTION

■ QUESTIONS ■

Your opinion

25 – 26 Did you enjoy reading this extract?   yes ☐   no ☐

Give reasons for your answer, describing what you did or did not like about the extract.

_____

_____

27 – 28 What do you think made Edmund keep on going although his journey across country was very hard?

_____

29 – 30 Do you think Edmund was frightened when he got to the Witch's House? If so, what do you think it was that frightened him?

_____

31 – 32 Would you like to have been on this adventure instead of Edmund? Give a reason for your answer.

_____

_____

33 – 34 Do you think the cold, the snow and the silence are important in this part of Edmund's adventure? Give a reason for your answer.

_____

_____

TEST 2

Pirate Story

Three of us afloat in the meadow by the swing,
Three of us aboard in the basket on the lea,
Winds are in the air, they are blowing in the spring,
And waves are on the meadow like the waves there are at sea.

Where shall we adventure, today that we're afloat,
Wary of the weather and steering by a star?
Shall it be to Africa, a-steering of the boat,
To Providence, or Babylon, or off to Malabar?

Hi! but here's a squadron a-rowing on the sea –
Cattle on the meadow a-charging with a roar!
Quick and we'll escape them, they're mad as they can be,
The wicket is the harbour and the garden is the shore.

by Robert Louis Stevenson

TEST 2   COMPREHENSION: FICTION

■ QUESTIONS ■

1 Who do you think is speaking in this poem?
   _____

2 What makes you think this?
   _____

3 What is the imaginary boat?
   a box ☐   a basket ☐   an old log ☐

4 What time of year is it? _____

5 The **waves on the meadow** are
   a flood of water from a stream ☐
   long grasses that are moving in the wind ☐   drifts of snow ☐

6 **Wary of the weather** means
   watchful in case the weather changes ☐
   enjoying the weather ☐   ignoring the weather ☐

7 How do you know that the child is pretending that it is night-time?
   _____

8 What is the **squadron a-rowing on the sea**?
   _____

9 – 10 What did the "sailors" do when the cows charged?
   _____

COMPREHENSION: NON-FICTION

TEST 3

Lifesavers of the RNLI

DANGER!
The oceans and seas are always moving because of the tides and the weather. We know when the tides are going to change, but the weather around the British Isles can change suddenly and dramatically. Anyone near or on the seas around our coasts can find themselves in great danger in a matter of minutes. Many people have lost their lives in terrible storms and accidents at sea.

HELP AT LAST
In 1824, the RNLI (Royal National Lifeboat Institution) was formed to help people in trouble at sea.

One story in particular caught the public's attention. On a stormy night in 1838, Grace Darling and her father saved the lives of nine men, women and children in a daring rescue from the wild seas of the Farne Islands.

In 1851 there was a national competition for a lifeboat design. The winner designed a self-righting lifeboat, and this idea was used for the next 50 years. This important invention kept the lifeboat crews safer. Steam was being used to power the new factories, and in 1890 the first steam-powered lifeboat was launched.

SAVING LIVES

Since 1869 the RNLI has saved the lives of more than 120,000 people. In 1990 alone, nearly 5,000 calls for help were answered. Because we live in a group of islands, nowhere in Britain is more than 75 miles from the sea. At this very moment, a lifeboat may be out on a rescue mission.

BRAVE CREWS

Lifeboats are crewed by volunteers: men and women who are good sailors and brave enough to risk their lives for others but who get no payment for this service. They all have other jobs, but they are on call at any time of the day or night. They can be called out in any weather to face any kind of danger. But the running of Britain's 210 lifeboat stations needs teams of people. There are volunteers who run the stations, maintain the boats and raise funds locally – most of the RNLI's funding comes from the public. Coastguards and the land-based emergency services are sometimes needed to help with rescues.

FAST RESPONSE

Lifeboat design has advanced tremendously in the last hundred years, and there is a lifeboat suitable for every kind of rescue. There are 13 different "classes", all of which have the fastest engines available. Some are moored afloat, and some need to be launched down a slipway.

In 1963 the first inflatable was used. These are popular for inshore rescue, especially in shallow waters. The children's television programme "Blue Peter" has organised many appeals and has bought several inflatable boats for the RNLI.

YOU CAN HELP
If you want to learn more about the work of the RNLI you can join the fundraising children's club "Stormforce". New members of the club receive an exciting pack containing a copy of *Stormforce News*, a membership badge, a certificate and some posters.

Write to:
>Stormforce HQ
>RNLI
>West Quay Road
>Poole
>Dorset BH15 1HZ

IT COULD BE YOU!
The RNLI rescues people in many different situations. For example, a fishing boat may capsize in a storm, a sailing yacht may lose a mast in a high wind, a child's dinghy may be blown out of its depth, or a lone sailor may be taken ill aboard his boat. Danger on the sea comes in many forms, but the RNLI is always ready, always fast and always brave. Remember, one of *your* family could be that person in need.

TEST 3   COMPREHENSION: NON-FICTION

■ **QUESTIONS** ■

1   The oceans and seas of the world are always
    moving ☐   still ☐   flat ☐

2   Many people have lost their lives in
    lifeboats ☐   terrible storms and accidents at sea ☐

3   The RNLI was formed   to help people in trouble at sea ☐
    to collect money for boats ☐   to help the crews ☐

4   Where does the RNLI get most of its money from?
    _____

5   A **volunteer** crew member is someone who is
    _____

6 – 7   Which other services sometimes help with rescues?
    _____

8   Which type of boat is suitable for inshore rescue in shallow waters?
    _____

9   Which club could you join to find out more about the RNLI?
    _____

10 If you join "Stormforce", what will you receive?
    _____
    _____
    _____

11 Name one dangerous situation at sea which may result in people needing to be rescued.
    _____

TEST 4

Is this the beast of Craigside?

The farming community around Craigside Castle is becoming increasingly alarmed. Eight sheep have been killed and two seriously injured during the last two weeks.

There have been six sightings of a large creature in the area during this time. Jamie Argyll saw it last Monday evening at about 7 o'clock.

"It was lurking in the long bracken behind the old barn at my farm, but it ran off as I approached," said Jamie.

Fiona McLeod said, "I've never seen anything like it! When it growled, it was louder than a crack of thunder!"

Fiona's sister added, "I think it must have escaped from a zoo."

After finding two of his best young sheep slaughtered, Sandy McNiven said, "The creature that did this must have claws like daggers."

The police have organised a search for the creature, and a reward of £500 has been offered for any information that leads to its capture.

Local wildlife ranger Angus McTigue said, "From what we have got so far, I think the creature could turn out to be a large wildcat."

TEST 4   COMPREHENSION: NON-FICTION

THE WILDCAT

The Latin name for the wildcat is *felis silvestris*. The name for the Scottish subspecies is *felis silvestris Grampia*. The Scottish wildcat produces two litters of kittens a year in May and August, and occasionally a third litter in December or January.

Most wildcats have striped tabby coats, but sometimes they interbreed with domestic cats so there can be great variations. Descendants of domestic cats which have turned wild may increase considerably in size, and become as fierce as the true wildcat.

Wildcats are meat eaters, and their diet consists of rats, mice, rabbits and small birds. They prefer to live and hunt alone (except during the breeding season).

■ QUESTIONS ■

1 – 8   From the report on page 17, select four sentences which are presented as facts and four sentences which are presented as the opinions of characters.

Facts

COMPREHENSION: NON-FICTION　　　TEST 4

Opinions

These questions are about the information on page 18.

9 What colour is a wildcat's coat? _____

10 How many litters of kittens does a wildcat have each year?

11 The Latin name for the Scottish wildcat is

　 felis silvestris ☐　*felis domesticus* ☐　*felis silvestris Grampia* ☐

12 What do wildcats prey on?

TEST 5

WELCOME TO CRAIGSIDE CASTLE

CASTLE OF THE YEAR 1996

Situated on the A523, 1.5 miles west of Seacombe

Take the No.7 bus from Seacombe to Muckleford

Open all year round except Christmas Day
Castle 12.00 noon to 5.00 p.m.
Gardens 1.00 a.m. to 6.00 p.m.
Guided tours every half-hour from 12.00 noon
Last admission 4.00 p.m.

See the falcons fly!
2.00 p.m. and 3.00 p.m.

ADMISSION		
Castle and gardens	Adult £3.00	Child £1.50
Gardens only	Adult £1.00	Child £0.50

Mini-Golf Course   Gift Shop   Giant Maze

Adventure Playground   Nature Trail   Dungeon Tea Rooms

Special Events This Year

CRAFT FAIR June 6th and 7th   VINTAGE CAR RALLY August 15th - 18th

COMPREHENSION: NON-FICTION   TEST 5

■ QUESTIONS ■

1 For how many hours each day is the castle open? _____

2 Where is the castle situated?
   _____

3 At which times do the falcons fly?
   _____

4 Which award did the castle win?
   _____

5 How much does it cost to visit the castle and the gardens?

   Adult _____   Child _____

6 – 9 List four outdoor attractions at Craigside Castle.

   _____   _____

   _____   _____

10 Which bus do you take from Seacombe to get to the castle?

   No.4 ☐   No.9 ☐   No.5 ☐   No.7 ☐   No.6 ☐

11 Which special events are advertised?
   _____   _____

12 At which time is the last admission to the castle?

   2.00 p.m. ☐   6.00 p.m. ☐   3.00 p.m. ☐   4.00 p.m. ☐

13 On which day is the castle closed?
   _____

21

Writing

STORY WRITING

TEST 6

Choose one of the ideas below as a starting point for writing a story. Use the boxes on page 23 to note down some of your ideas for the story. Spend 10–15 minutes on Test 6 (planning your story) and then move on to Test 7 (writing your story).

A   You are visiting a castle where you get lost in a maze of corridors. As you search for a way out, you accidentally lean against a carved panel which swings open to reveal a secret passage. Write a story about what happens.

B   You are listening to the local radio station when suddenly the programme is interrupted by an SOS message. A storm is raging and some people on a yacht are in danger of drowning. You just have time to scribble details of their position before your radio aerial is hit by the storm. Write a story about what you do next.

C   You are a keen nature lover. One day, while visiting your local beauty spot, you overhear a conversation between two officials discussing plans for a new factory to be built there. It is the only woodland in the area. Write a story about what you do next and whose help you seek.

STORY WRITING   TESTS 6/7

■ **STORY PLANNING** ■

Title
_____

1 – 2   Setting (Where and when does it happen?)
_____
_____

3 – 4   Characters (Who are they? What are they like?)
_____
_____

5 – 6   How does the story begin?
_____
_____

7 – 8   What is the main event?
_____
_____

9 – 10   How does the story end?
_____
_____

■ **STORY WRITING** ■

TEST 7

1 – 10   Now write your story on a sheet of paper.

LETTER WRITING

TEST 8

Choose one of the ideas below as a starting point for writing a letter. Use the boxes on page 25 to make notes about what you want to say in your letter. Spend 5–10 minutes on Test 8 (planning your letter) and then move on to Test 9 (writing your letter).

A   You are on an adventure holiday, and you write a letter home telling of all the exciting things you have done since you arrived.

B   One of your favourite children's television programmes is about to be taken off the air. The presenter has invited children to write to the television company to ask for the show to be saved. Write a letter, giving as many reasons as you can for the programme to continue.

C   You have a penfriend who lives in another country. Write a letter inviting them to stay with you for a holiday. Tell them about all the things you will do and the exciting places you will visit. Draw on your own real experiences.

D   Your favourite band is due to appear at the local theatre, and there is a competition to win four free tickets and the chance to go backstage. All you have to do is to write a letter to the manager of the theatre, saying why you like the band and why you would like to meet them, and listing three questions you would like to ask them.

LETTER WRITING   TESTS 8/9

■ **LETTER PLANNING** ■

1 – 2 Who will you address the letter to?

3 – 5 How will the letter begin?

6 – 8 What do you want to say in your letter? Make some notes here.

9 – 10 How will you end your letter?

■ **LETTER WRITING** ■

TEST 9

1 – 10 Now write your letter on a sheet of paper.

25

SPELLING

TEST 10

1 – 55   Listen carefully the first time this story is read to you. As it is read for the second time, fill in the missing words, making sure you spell them correctly.

The Golden Eagle

"I've got a golden eagle. I keep it _____ home. I have to feed it raw meat or it _____ upset!" Davy looked smug as he told Mike his latest _____. "I hold it on my fist and feed it lumps of _____," he added, holding his arm outstretched to _____ his friend.

Mike looked at him thoughtfully. He wasn't _____ whether to believe Davy. He always came up with good _____, but that's just what they were – stories, from his _____ imagination. "What's it like, then?" he _____ suspiciously.

This was just what Davy had been hoping for. "Well, it's got _____ talons, and each of its feet is as big as my _____. Its legs are feathered but its feet are _____ of yellow and scaly like a dinosaur _____ have had. Its feathers are dark _____ all over except for a golden tinge to its head. Like the sun on top of a _____." Davy smiled as he described it, and his _____ became dreamy.

"What's its _____ like? Has it got teeth as big as your fingers?" Mike _____, but Davy was serious.

"Birds don't have teeth, silly. Its beak is huge — _____ and curved, and so sharp it can tear raw meat from the _____. Wait until you see it."

Mike _____ to look scared. "Well, I hope my bones are safe. Aren't those birds dangerous or _____?" he asked, _____ believing Davy now.

TEST 10   SPELLING

"You're too skinny!" laughed Davy. "They're very _____ to their prey. Look out if you're a _____, a hare, a grouse or even a little _____."

Mike laughed. "My Mum says I'm a little lamb." He pursed his lips and _____ to look lamb-like. He wondered how big the eagle _____. Could it fit in a shed, or did it need a huge _____ like the ones at the bird rescue place they had visited with their _____?

Davy went on describing the golden eagle. It has a wingspan of two metres, and _____ its eyrie, which is the name of its nest, out of piles of _____ and twigs. Not too comfy for the nestlings, _____ Mike. Eagles build their eyries about 500 metres above sea level on _____ in Scotland. The pair (the _____ and the female) repair their nest in November and December. Mike was _____ that it must be quite snowy in the Highlands.

"They _____ a clutch of eggs in March or April," Davy went on knowledgeably. He _____ as if he'd swallowed an encyclopaedia. "There are

SPELLING   TEST 10

_____ only two eggs, white with red-brown markings."

Davy had _____ Mike's interest now, and he looked at his _____ with respect. "Well, I'd certainly like to see your _____ eagle. How did you get it? I thought they were very _____."

Davy drew him down the garden path towards the shed. "_____ are, and my Dad paid a lot for this one. It's 50 years old," he said, opening the door to the _____.

Mike held his _____. Would it attack him? He winced in case it _____ too loudly.

"Well, what do you think? Isn't it a _____?" breathed Davy, with a _____ sweep of his arm in the direction of his _____ workbench. A fierce eye stared at _____ from the gloom, and Mike held his _____.

"Why _____ it move?" he whispered from _____ Davy's back.

"Stuffed birds don't move ..." Davy _____ resist a smirk.

29

HANDWRITING

TEST 11

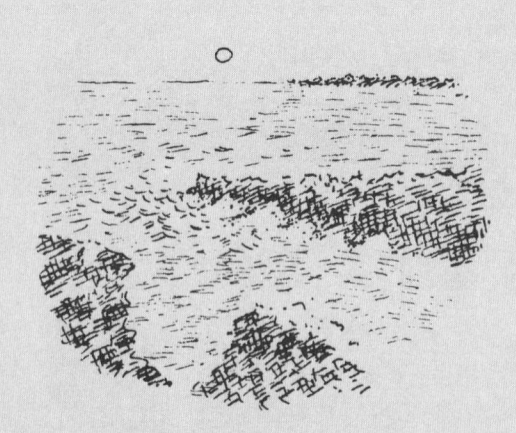

The Eagle

He clasps the crag with crooked hands;
Close to the sun in lonely lands,
Ringed with the azure world, he stands.

The wrinkled sea beneath him crawls;
He watches from his mountain walls,
And like a thunderbolt he falls.

by Alfred Lord Tennyson

Copy this poem carefully, in your best handwriting.

ANSWERS

Test 1

1. dark and snowy
2. on a journey
3. a full moon
4. a small castle
5. an enormous lion crouched as if it was ready to spring
6. Aslan
7. The wolf was alive, and rose to speak.
8. the White Witch
9. all he had heard before leaving the Beavers' house
10. King of Narnia
11. He drew on its face with a pencil, because he found that it was made of stone and couldn't harm him.
12. – 14 Any of the following:
    it lay across the threshold,
    it was huge,
    all the hair on its back was bristling,
    it opened its great red mouth,
    it had a growling voice,
    it ordered Edmund to stand still,
    it bounded back to him
15. – 16 Any of the following:
    unfriendly, bad-tempered, angry, cruel, suspicious, impatient, threatening, terrible
17. – 18 the weather and the darkness
19. – 21 the countryside, the courtyard and the long, gloomy hall
22. – 24 cold, still, stone
25. – 26 Either answer is valid as long as a good reason is given, and it is written as a complete sentence.
27. – 28 Any of the following:
    the thought of becoming King of Narnia,
    getting his own back on Peter,
    any other answer supported by something in the text
29. – 30 Any of the following:
    the stone lion, the real wolf, the changed manner of the Witch
31. – 32 Any answer is valid as long as a good reason is given, and it is written as a complete sentence.
33. – 34 Any answer is valid as long as a good reason is given, and it is written as a complete sentence.

Test 2

1. A child is speaking.
2. He or she is pretending to be in a ship.
3. a basket
4. spring
5. long grasses that are moving in the wind
6. watchful in case the weather changes
7. He or she talks of steering by a star, which would only be seen at night.
8. cattle on the meadow
9. – 10 They ran through a gate and into the garden.

Test 3

1. moving
2. terrible storms and accidents at sea
3. to help people in trouble at sea
4. the public
5. a good sailor and brave enough to risk their life for others, but who works without pay
6. – 7 coastguards and the land-based emergency services
8. an inflatable
9. "Stormforce"
10. an exciting pack containing a copy of *Stormforce News*, a membership badge, a certificate and some posters
11. Any of the following:
    a fishing boat may capsize in a storm,
    a sailing boat may lose a mast in a high wind,
    a child's dinghy may be blown out of its depth,
    a lone sailor may be taken ill aboard his boat

Test 4

1. – 4 Any of the following:
   Eight sheep have been killed and two seriously injured during the last two weeks.
   There have been six sightings of a large creature in the area during this time.

31

Jamie Argyll saw it last Monday evening at about 7 o'clock.
The police have organised a search for the creature, and a reward of £500 has been offered for any information that leads to its capture.

5 – 8   Any of the following:
When it growled, it was louder than a crack of thunder!
I think it must have escaped from a zoo.
The creature that did this must have claws like daggers.
From what we have got so far, I think the creature could turn out to be a large wildcat.

9   tabby
10 usually two, sometimes three
11 *felis silvestris Grampia*
12 rats, mice, rabbits and small birds

Test 5

1   5 hours
2   on the A523, 1.5 miles west of Seacombe
3   2.00 p.m. and 3.00 p.m.
4   Castle of the Year
5   £3.00   £1.50
6 – 9   Any of the following:
gardens, nature trail, giant maze, adventure playground, mini-golf course
10 No.7
11 a Craft Fair and a Vintage Car Rally
12 4.00 p.m.
13 Christmas Day

Tests 6 – 9   See notes on assessment (inside front cover).

Test 10

1 – 55   at   gets   news   meat   show   sure   stories   brilliant   asked   huge   hand   sort   might   brown   mountain   eyes   beak   laughed   powerful   bones   pretended   something   almost   dangerous   rabbit   lamb   tried   was   cage   school   builds   sticks   thought   mountainsides   male   thinking   lay   sounded   usually   caught   friend   golden   rare   They   shed   breath   screeched   beauty   majestic   Dad's   them   breath   doesn't   behind   couldn't

Copy these words on a separate piece of paper, then read out the story to your child, adding the missing words. Pause at the end of the sentence and repeat the word if necessary.

Test 11   See notes on assessment (inside front cover).

Text © Jim Fitzsimmons and
Rhona Whiteford 1997
The Lion, the Witch and the Wardrobe
by C.S. Lewis © the Estate of C.S.
Lewis 1950. Reproduced by permission
of HarperCollins Publishers Ltd.

Illustrations © John Eastwood 1997

The right of Jim Fitzsimmons and
Rhona Whiteford to be identified as the
authors of this work have been
asserted by them in accordance with
the Copyright, Design and Patents Act
1988.

First published in Great Britain 1997

All rights reserved. No part of this
publication may be reproduced, stored
in a retrieval system, or transmitted, in
any form or by any means, without the
prior written permission of the
publisher, nor be otherwise circulated
in any form of binding or cover other
than that in which it is published and
without a similar condition being
imposed on the subsequent purchaser.

Published by
Hodder Children's Books,
a division of Hodder Headline plc,
338 Euston Road, London NW1 3BH

Printed and bound in Great Britain

A CIP record is registered by and held
at the British Library.

The National Curriculum for Science is divided into three main elements: **Life processes and living things**, **Materials and their properties**, and **Physical processes**. The fourth element, **Experimental and investigative science**, underpins the other three. This chart lists the tests you will find in this book together with a range of marks that will help you to make a more informed assessment of your child's level of performance. The SATs are assessed by a trained marker, but your test results are valuable as a guide. The tests become more difficult as you work through the book.

These tests are just like the SATs, but remember that tests do not measure everything that children can do; the teacher will also make an assessment of performance over the whole year.

Test	Time allowed (minutes)	Marks	Assessment Total	C	B	A
Test Group 1						
1 Life processes and living things	15	28				
2 Materials and their properties	15	27				
3 Physical processes	15	15	90	5–30	31–65	66–90
4 Life processes and living things/ Materials and their properties/ Physical processes	30	20				
Test Group 2						
5 Life processes and living things	15	21				
6 Materials and their properties	15	24				
7 Physical processes	15	20	98	5–35	36–70	71–98
8 Life processes and living things/ Materials and their properties/ Physical processes	30	33				
Test Group 3						
9 Life processes and living things	15	22				
10 Materials and their properties	15	11				
11 Physical processes	15	18	100	5–40	41–64	65–100
12 Life processes and living things/ Materials and their properties/ Physical processes	30	49				

Key

C Your child has an average understanding of this area. Regular practice at home using workbooks will build their skills and confidence.

B Your child has a good understanding of this area, but further practice will improve their performance.

A Your child has a very good grasp of this area. Continued practice will help them achieve the best possible results.

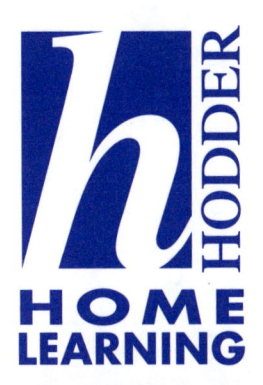

SATs Practice in Science

AGE 11

Rhona Whiteford and Jim Fitzsimmons
Illustrated by Sara Silcock

The National Curriculum for England and Wales requires all 11 year-olds in the final year of Primary school (Key Stage 2) to be tested in English, Mathematics and Science. These tests are called SATs (Standard Assessment Tasks), and are completed during the normal school day. There is a national timetable for the tests. Their purpose is to give schools information about what children are achieving compared to other of the same age, and to highlight areas where help is needed. This book will help you to prepare your child for the SATs in Science. Although the SATs are taken at age 11, this book may be used for practice throughout Year 6.

How to help your child

a Working together
If you work through each test with your child, you may discover areas where extra practice is needed.

b Test conditions
The SATs are timed at this stage, so you can use this book to prepare your child for real test conditions. Encourage them to work independently and with good concentration. The time allowed for each test is shown in the chart on the left, but do not be too strict about timing if your child is anxious. Do one test at a time, starting at the beginning of the book and working as far as you can through the three Test Groups (1, 2 and 3). Read each test together before your child starts to work through it.

Although Science is essentially a practical subject, it does require the collection and analysis of data, and the SATs reflect this aspect of an investigation.

- Keep sessions short and frequent, perhaps one test per day.

- Make sure you and your child are relaxed and have a quiet place in which to work.

- Avoid putting your child under pressure.

- Build your child's confidence by offering plenty of praise and encouragement.

Hodder Children's Books

The only home learning programme supported by the NCPTA

Life Processes and Living Things

TEST 1   Living and non-living things

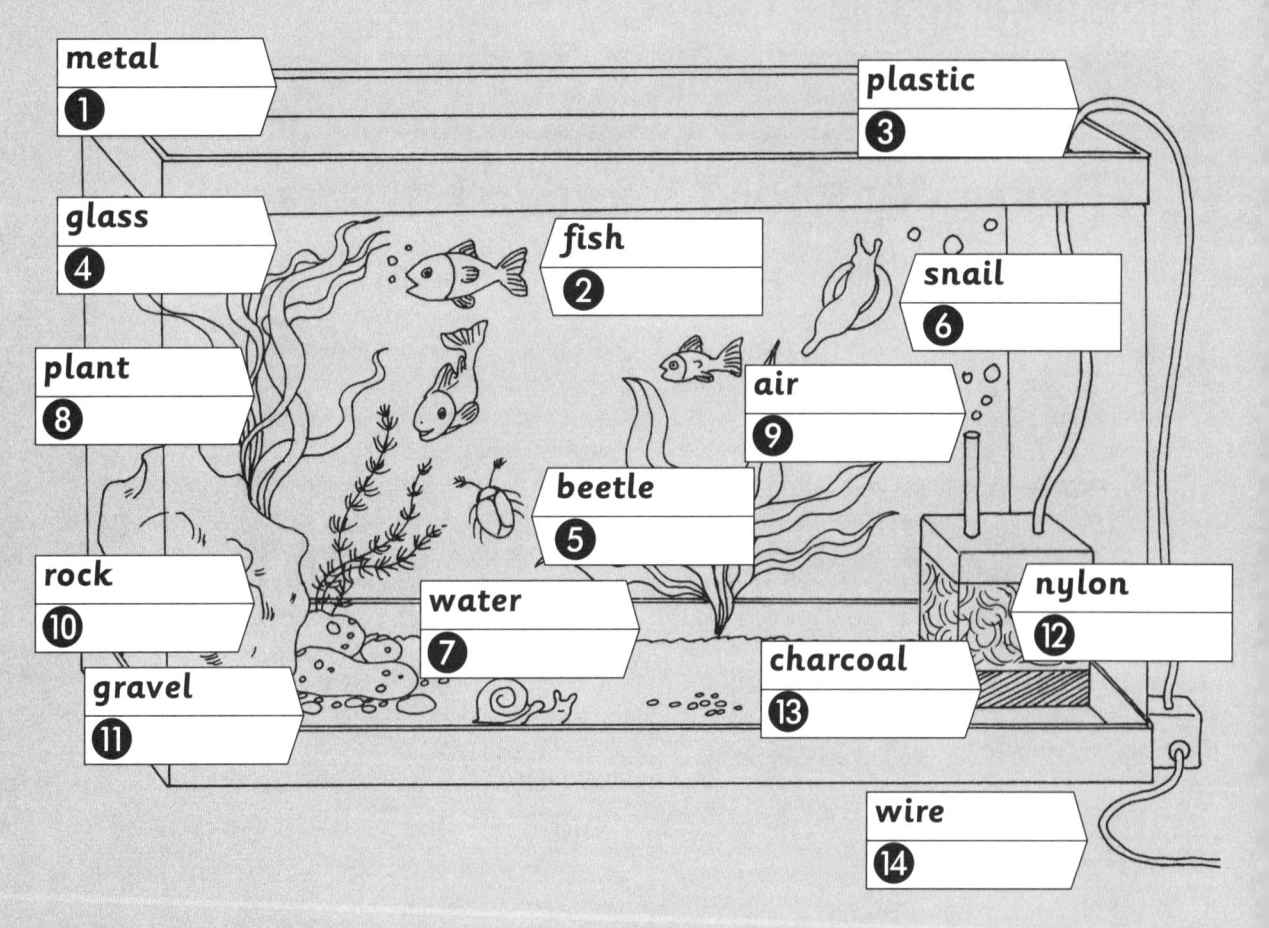

- metal ①
- plastic ③
- glass ④
- fish ②
- snail ⑥
- plant ⑧
- air ⑨
- beetle ⑤
- rock ⑩
- water ⑦
- nylon ⑫
- gravel ⑪
- charcoal ⑬
- wire ⑭

A fish tank contains a complete environment.

There are both living and non-living things in and around this fish tank. Write **living** or **non-living** on each label.

Do the living things need the non-living things? If so, give three examples.

⑮ – ⑯

⑰ – ⑱

⑲ – ⑳

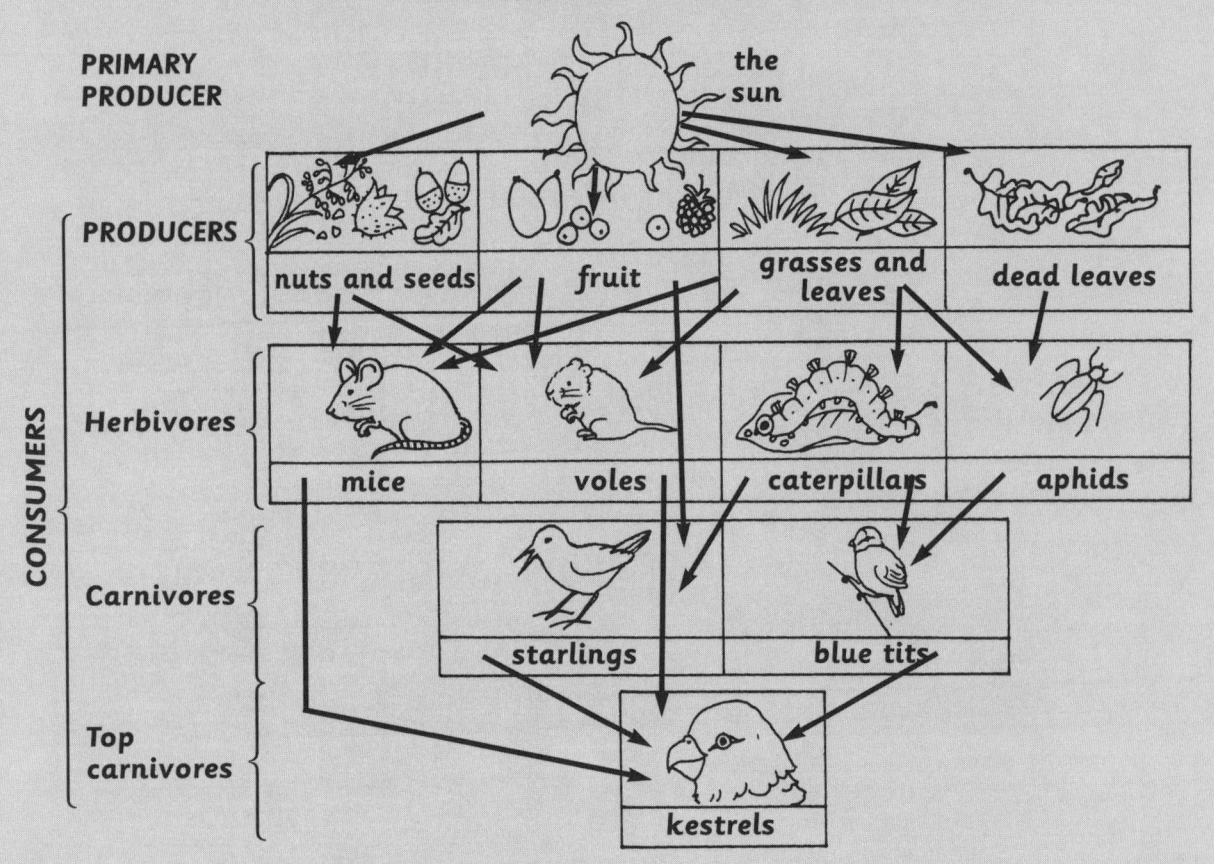

LIFE PROCESSES AND LIVING THINGS — TEST 1

A food web

PRIMARY PRODUCER: the sun

PRODUCERS: nuts and seeds, fruit, grasses and leaves, dead leaves

CONSUMERS:
- Herbivores: mice, voles, caterpillars, aphids
- Carnivores: starlings, blue tits
- Top carnivores: kestrels

21 Which is the most important food producer in this web?

22 Which animal is not eaten by any other in this web?

23 – 25 Why are nuts and seeds important to kestrels?

26 – 28 What do you think would happen if the producers were poisoned by chemicals?

Materials and their Properties

TEST 2   Choosing materials

Choose the most suitable material from the chart below for making each part of this roller boot. Write your answers on the labels.

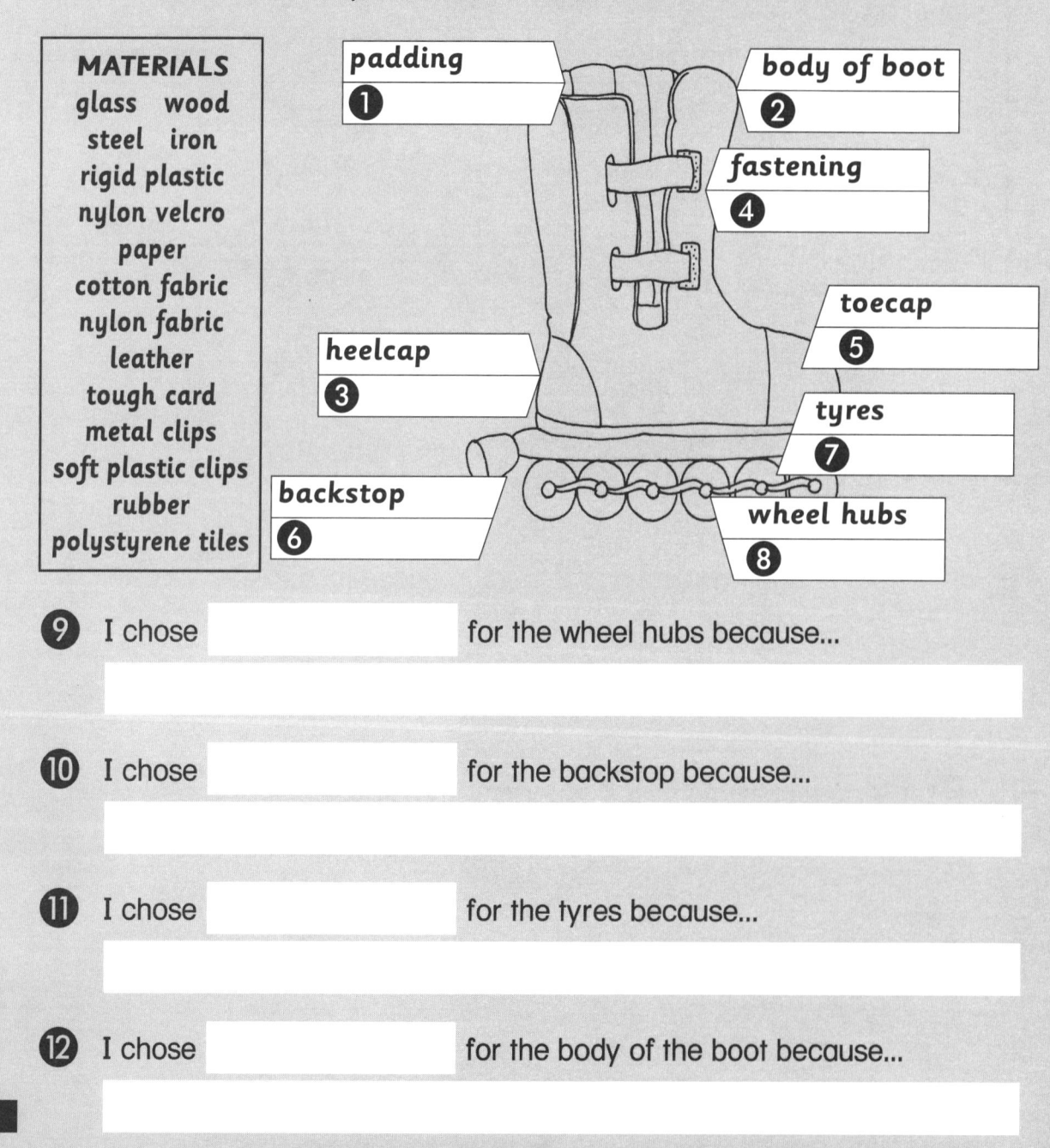

MATERIALS
glass   wood
steel   iron
rigid plastic
nylon velcro
paper
cotton fabric
nylon fabric
leather
tough card
metal clips
soft plastic clips
rubber
polystyrene tiles

padding ❶

body of boot ❷

fastening ❹

heelcap ❸

toecap ❺

backstop ❻

tyres ❼

wheel hubs ❽

❾ I chose _____ for the wheel hubs because...

❿ I chose _____ for the backstop because...

⓫ I chose _____ for the tyres because...

⓬ I chose _____ for the body of the boot because...

MATERIALS AND THEIR PROPERTIES   TEST 2

Dissolving and melting

13 – 16 Which of these materials dissolve in cold water? Tick the boxes.

sugar ☐   sand ☐   salt ☐   instant coffee ☐

chocolate ☐   chalk ☐   icing sugar ☐   rubber ☐

What would happen if you put each of these materials in a pan and heated it gently?

17 chocolate _____
18 sand _____
19 wax _____
20 butter _____
21 ice _____
22 water _____

23 – 27 If someone spilled sugar on the new gravel for your fish tank, how would you separate the two materials? Write and draw your answer.

Physical Processes

TEST 3 Floating and sinking

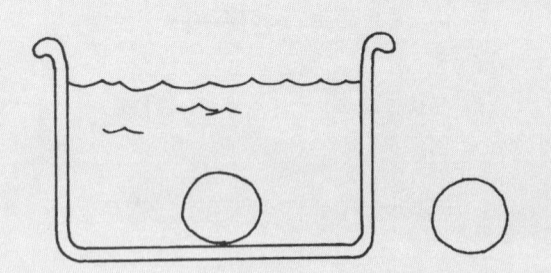

Each of these two Plasticine balls has a mass of 300g. The first ball sank when it was put into the water.

❶ – ❸ Could the second ball be made to float? If so, how?

❹ – ❺ Which two forces are acting on a floating object?

Sound

Dave is playing the drum.

❻ What happens to the drum when it is hit by the drumstick?

❼ How could you prove it?

❽ What does sound travel through to reach our ears?

PHYSICAL PROCESSES   TEST 3

Electrical circuits

9 Which of these circuits will light the bulb?

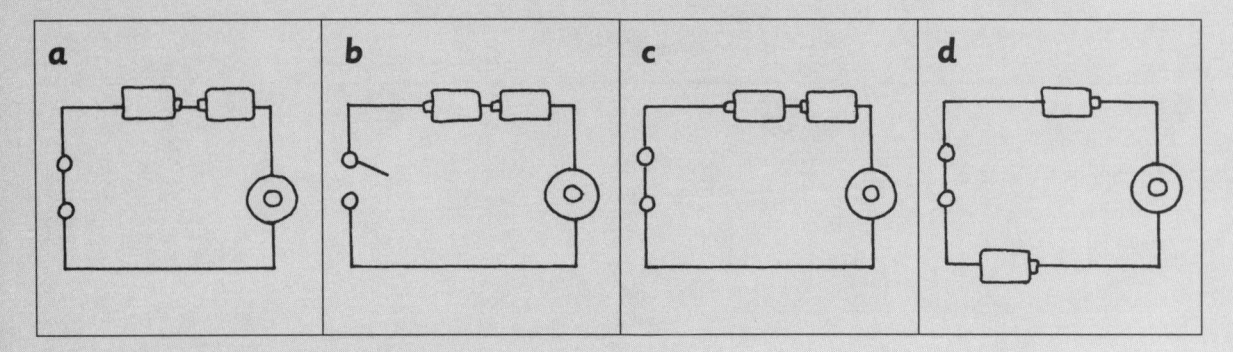

a   b   c   d

10 – 12 Draw a circuit that will light a bulb. You can use only one battery.

Magnetism

Magnets have opposite poles, north and south. Look at this picture.

13 Will this toy car be pushed along by the child's hand-held magnet?   Yes   No

14 – 15 Why?

7

Life Processes and Living Things/ Materials and their Properties/ Physical Processes

TEST 4   Light

Draw the light source ☼ in each picture.

❶   **❷**   **❸**

These two pictures show a street scene at 8.30 p.m. One picture shows the scene in winter, and the other shows the scene in summer. Which is which?

a   b

❹ **Picture a** shows the street in _____ .

❺ **Picture b** shows the street in _____ .

❻ What is the reason for the difference?

8

LIFE PROCESSES/MATERIALS/PHYSICAL PROCESSES   TEST 4

Air

Wind is moving air. Look at this picture. Name three things which are moved by the wind.

7 _____
8 _____
9 _____

a   a screwed-up sheet of paper   *b*   a flat sheet of paper

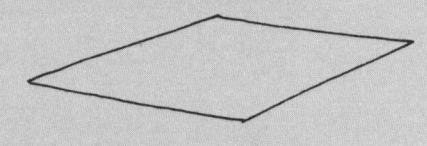

10   If both sheets of paper were dropped from the same height, which sheet of paper would fall more slowly?

11   Why?
_____

12   How could you make the other sheet of paper fall more slowly?
_____

TEST 4   LIFE PROCESSES/MATERIALS/PHYSICAL PROCESSES

Old and young

parent   **baby**    **toddler**    **teenager**

⑬ – ⑮ Complete this diagram to show the life cycle of a human being.

parent

Staying healthy

Here are Ace Baseline and Biff Volley, two top tennis players. They want to be the best, so they must stay fit and healthy. They decide that smoking is bad for them.

⑯ Give a reason.

⑰ Just being near someone who is smoking can damage your health. How?

LIFE PROCESSES / MATERIALS / PHYSICAL PROCESSES   TEST 4

Insulation

Four boiled eggs were placed in four equal-sized plastic sandwich boxes while they were still hot. Three of the boxes were packed with different materials. The fourth box contained only the egg.

wool   sand   newspaper   no material

After half an hour the eggs were removed to see how hot they were. This chart shows the results.

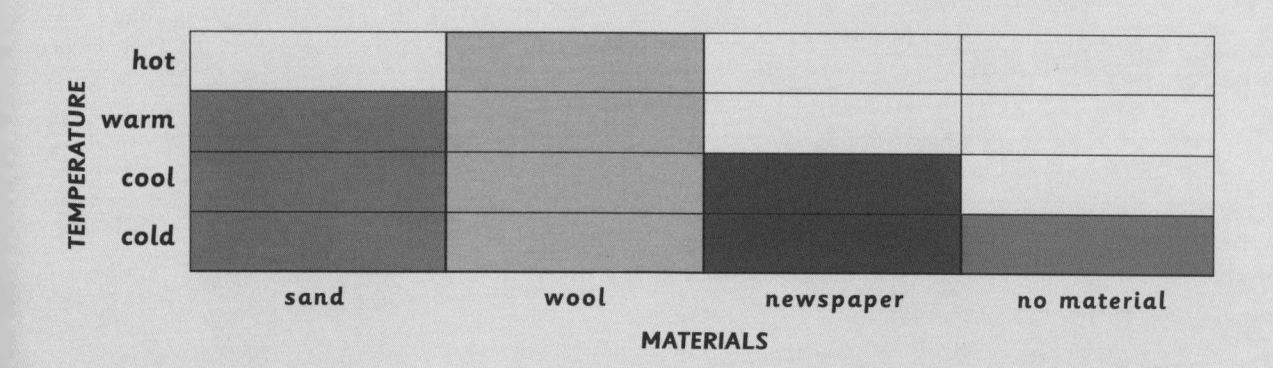

18 Which material kept the egg hottest?

19 Why was the empty box not very good at keeping the egg hot?

20 Why is it best to use layers of material to keep things hot?

Life Processes and Living Things

TEST 5

The human body

Name these organs.

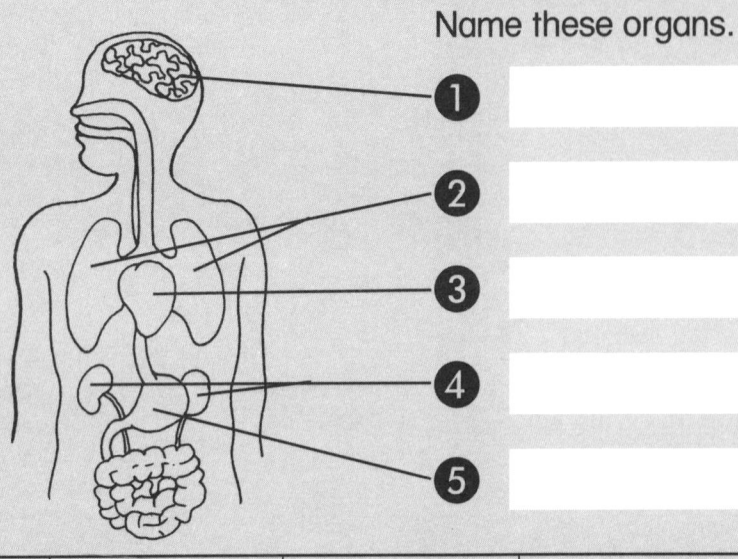

1.
2.
3.
4.
5.

| heart | lungs | stomach | kidneys | brain |

Exercise and rest

Look at these pictures.

sleeping   reading   running

6 – 8 Which activity makes the heart beat the most slowly?

Why?

Which activity makes the heart beat the most quickly?

Why?

LIFE PROCESSES AND LIVING THINGS   TEST 5

Plants

Look at these plants.

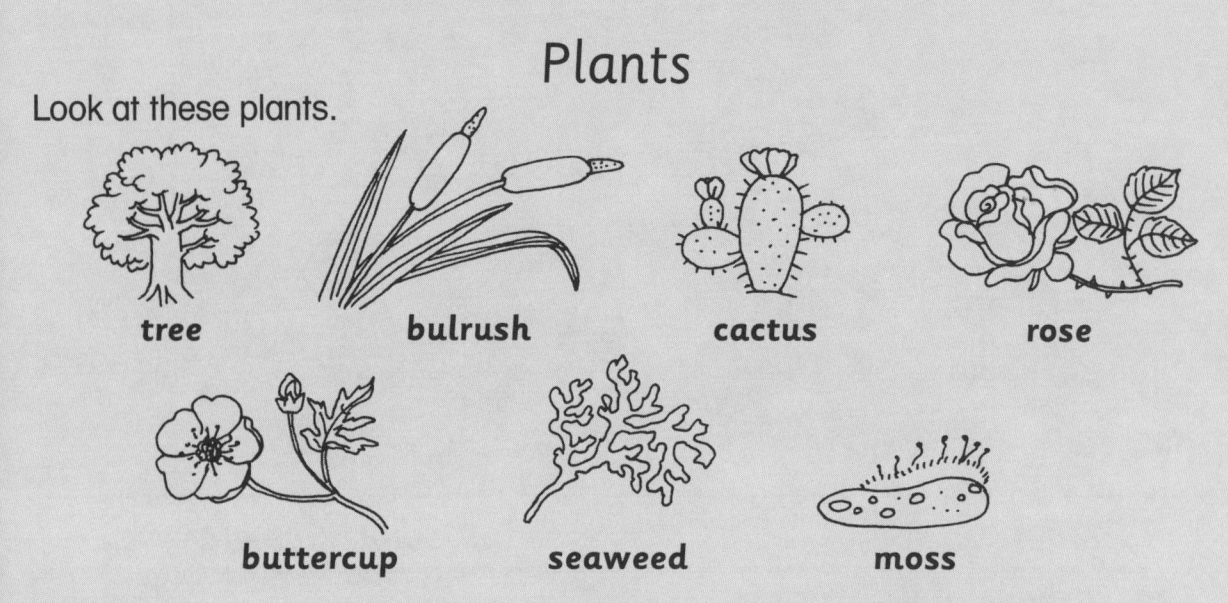

- tree
- bulrush
- cactus
- rose
- buttercup
- seaweed
- moss

Write the name of each plant underneath the name of the place where it might grow.

in a desert	in a forest	in a garden	under the sea
⑨	⑩	⑪	⑫

in a meadow	on a wall	in a marsh
⑬	⑭	⑮

Which three things do house plants need in order to grow?

⑯ _____   ⑰ _____   ⑱ _____

What would happen to a house plant under the following conditions?

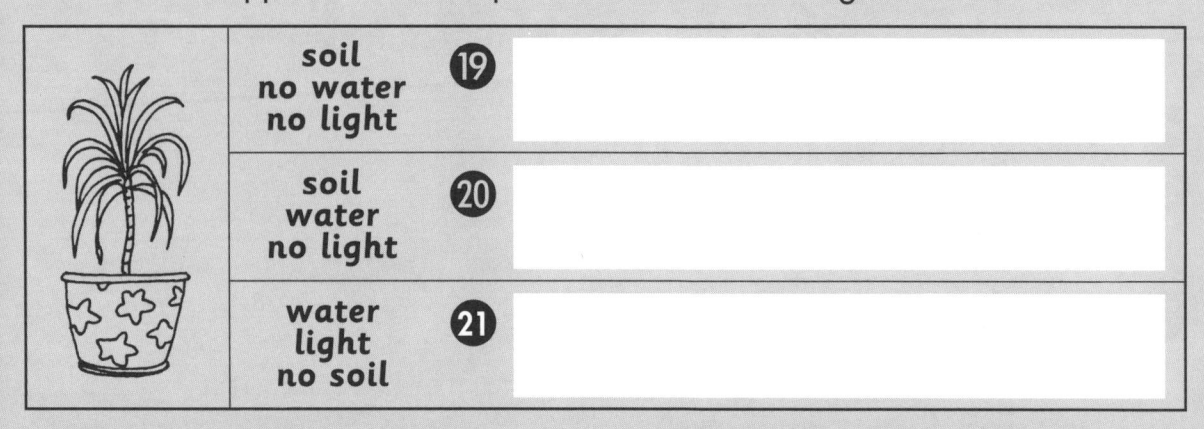

	soil no water no light	⑲
	soil water no light	⑳
	water light no soil	㉑

Materials and their Properties

TEST 6 — Solids, liquids and gases

solid 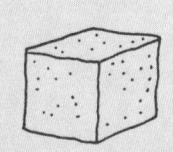   liquid    gas

① – ⑯ Tick the boxes to show the properties of solids, liquids and gases.

Properties	Solid	Liquid	Gas
has a shape of its own			
keeps this shape			
can be poured			
finds its own level			
can be squashed into a smaller space			
floats above ground			
falls to the ground when dropped			
flows through a tube			
can be transparent/translucent or opaque			

A certain substance is ...

... liquid   ... colourless   ... tasteless

...needed daily by plants and animals

⑰ The substance is ▭

⑱ How can this liquid be made into a solid?

⑲ How can it be made into a gas?

MATERIALS AND THEIR PROPERTIES — TEST 6

Testing strength

Some children carried out a test to see which of five supermarket carrier bags was the strongest. They used a spring balance and some large pebbles.

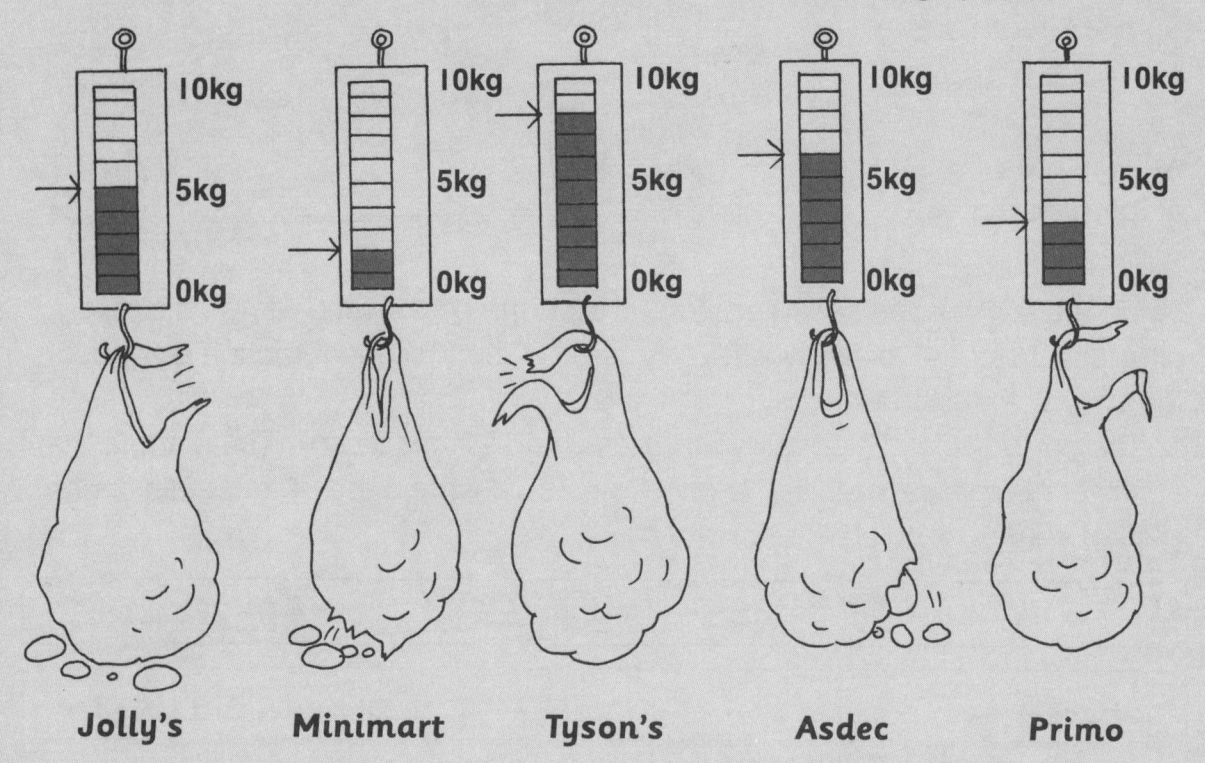

Jolly's	Minimart	Tyson's	Asdec	Primo
5kg	3kg	7kg	6kg	4kg

The bags broke when the weight of the pebbles was too great for their strength. The top weight each bag could carry is recorded on the balances. The point at which the bag split is also shown.

20 Which bag was the weakest?

21 Which bag was the strongest?

22 Which part of the bags split?

23 Which were the two strongest bags?

24 How could supermarkets improve their bags?

Physical Processes

TEST 7

Friction

Some children wanted to find out how far a toy car would roll on different surfaces.

Using the same slope each time, they rolled the car down a ramp on to six different surfaces, to see which surface produced the least friction and so let the car roll the furthest.

The car travelled 25cm on short grass, and 12 cm on soil. Think about the other four surfaces listed in the chart, and then write each of these distances in what you judge to be the correct box.

| ❶ 5 m | ❷ 2 cm | ❸ 1.5 m | ❹ 20 cm |

Surface	Distance travelled
smooth wooden floor	
short grass	25 cm
deep-pile carpet	
smooth PE mat	
rough concrete path	
soil	12 cm

❺ What is the force that provided resistance and slowed the car down?

❻ Which surface provided the most friction?

❼ Which surface provided the least friction?

❽ What is the force that pulled the car down the slope?

PHYSICAL PROCESSES TEST 7

9 – 13 On the smooth wooden floor, two similar cars were rolled down the same slope. One weighed 250g, and the other weighed 550g. One travelled 6.25m, and one travelled 3.91m. Which do you think was which, and why?

Space

Look at this picture.

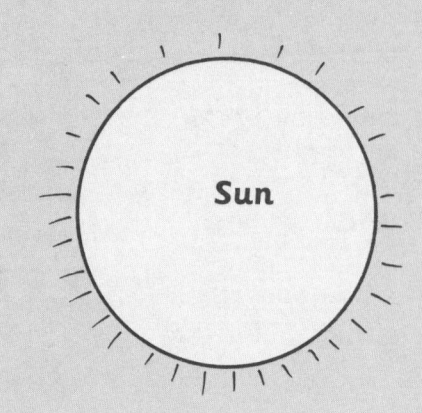

Moon   Earth   Sun

14 Why is a shadow covering the Moon?

15 This situation is called

| an ellipse | an orbit | a circuit |
| a sunspot | a sunset | an eclipse |

16 The Moon orbits the _____.

17 It takes the _____ 365 days to orbit the Sun.

18 The _____ turns on its axis every 24 hours.

Look at this picture.

Sun   UK

19 Is it day or night in the UK?

20 Shade the part of the Earth where it is night.

Life Processes and Living Things/ Materials and their Properties/ Physical Processes

TEST 8 — Food for energy

Look at these meals.

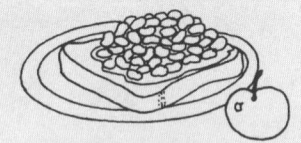

a beans on toast/ an apple

b a pork steak, salad, baked potatoes/treacle pudding, custard

c a hot dog, chips, crisps/ chocolate pudding

d a hamburger/ a bar of chocolate

e ham salad, pasta/ an apple, a banana

1 Which meal would give enough energy to a person who does heavy outdoor work?

2 Which meal is the most unbalanced and contains too much fat?

3 Which meals contain plenty of vitamins and fibre?

4 Which meals would be the most healthy lunches for a child?

The human body – what organs do

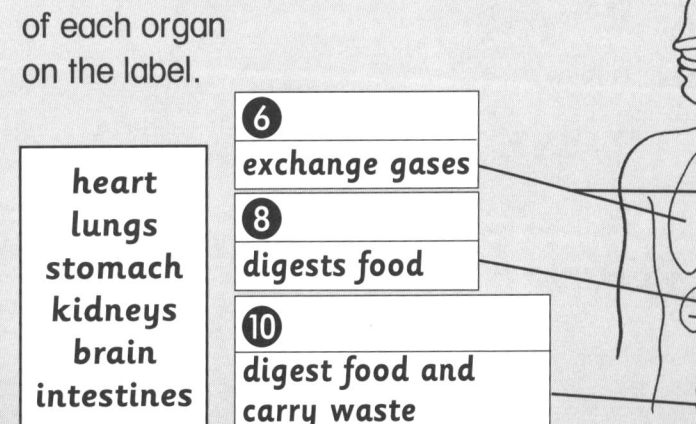

Write the name of each organ on the label.

heart
lungs
stomach
kidneys
brain
intestines

5 controls movement and functions

6 exchange gases

7 pumps blood

8 digests food

9 filter blood

10 digest food and carry waste

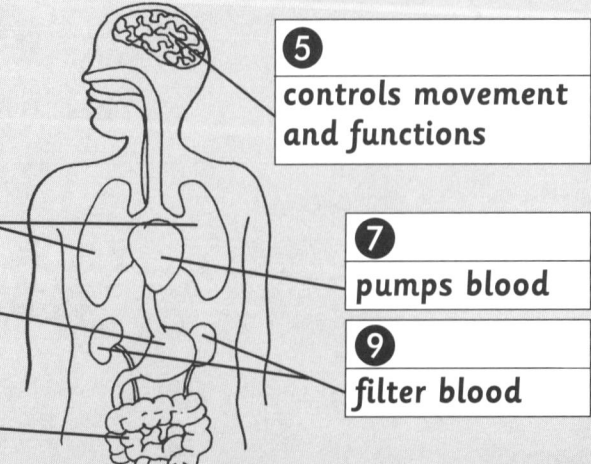

LIFE PROCESSES/MATERIALS/PHYSICAL PROCESSES TEST 8

Light

a

b

Sue can look at her face in the mirror, but can she look behind her without turning round?

11–12 Draw a mirror on **Picture a** and draw arrows to show the direction of the light rays from Sue's eyes to the mirror and back.

13–14 Draw a mirror on **Picture b** and draw arrows to show the direction of the light rays from Sue's eyes to the mirror and then to the flowers and back.

Complete this sentence to show the path in which light travels.

15–16 Light travels in _____ _____ .

Periscopes are used for looking round corners or over obstacles. Sue is using one to look at this flower.

17 Draw arrows to show the path of light.

How can the torch shine its light on the flowers without pointing at them?

18 Draw arrows to show the path of light.

TEST 8   LIFE PROCESSES/MATERIALS/PHYSICAL PROCESSES

Seed dispersal

Seeds are spread from plants in several ways: by the wind, by animals or by the explosion of the seed pod.
Here are some seeds.

burdock   strawberry   pea

dandelion   beech   sycamore

Write the name of each plant in the correct box.

19   seeds spread by wind

20   seeds spread by animals

21   seeds spread by the explosion of the seed pod

22   Why is it important that the seeds are spread from the parent plant?

23   How are burrs from the burdock plant spread by animals?

LIFE PROCESSES/MATERIALS/PHYSICAL PROCESSES   TEST 8

Separating materials

Four of these words describe ways of separating mixtures of materials. Write them down.

㉔ _____

㉕ _____

㉖ _____

㉗ _____

> slicing   breaking
> sieving
> chopping   evaporating
> filtering   chromatography

Some cooking ingredients have got mixed up.

a peas and salt

b ground pepper and water

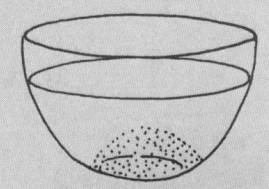

c salt and water

How would you separate the materials in each mixture?
What equipment would you need?

㉘ – ㉙ a _____

㉚ – ㉛ b _____

㉜ – ㉝ c _____

Life Processes and Living Things

TEST 9 Parts of a plant

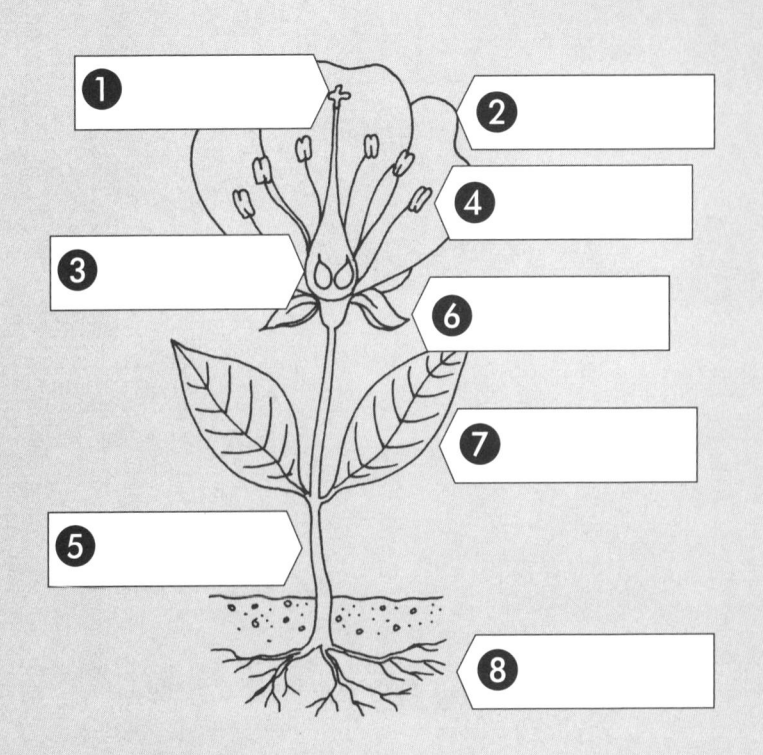

① ② ③ ④ ⑤ ⑥ ⑦ ⑧

petal
leaf
stamen
stigma
root
sepal
ovary
stem

Which of these parts ...

⑨ makes food for the plant?

⑩ takes in water and food for the plant?

⑪ makes the seeds which will grow into new plants?

⑫ makes and stores pollen?

⑬ attracts the insects which are needed to pollinate the plant?

⑭ protects the flower when it is a bud?

⑮ supports the flower and the leaves?

⑯ is sticky so that the pollen sticks to it?

LIFE PROCESSES AND LIVING THINGS — TEST 9

Classifying animals

Animals are divided into two groups:

Animals with a backbone	Animals without a backbone

Those with a backbone are further divided into:

Mammals	Fish	Reptiles	Birds	Amphibians

Decide which sub-group of animals each of these descriptions fits, and write its name in the box.

- is warm-blooded
- has hair or fur
- breathes air into its lungs
- has teeth
- suckles its young

17

- is warm-blooded
- has feathers
- has two legs
- lays eggs
- has wings
- has no teeth

18

- is cold-blooded
- breathes through its gills
- has scales
- lives in water

19

- is cold-blooded
- has scales
- breathes air into its lungs
- lays eggs

20

- is cold-blooded
- has smooth skin
- has lungs but absorbs air into its skin
- lays eggs

21

Which of these animals is a fish?

22 shark   dolphin

23

Materials and their Properties

TEST 10 Soil

Clay is composed of small particles, and water cannot pass through it easily. Soil is composed of larger particles, and water can pass through it fairly easily. Gravel is composed of large particles, and water can pass through it very easily.

A group of children took four funnels. They filled one with clay, one with gravel, one with a mixture of soil and clay, and one with a mixture of soil and gravel. They passed the same amount of water through each funnel, and after five minutes they recorded how much water had passed through.

This bar chart shows their results.

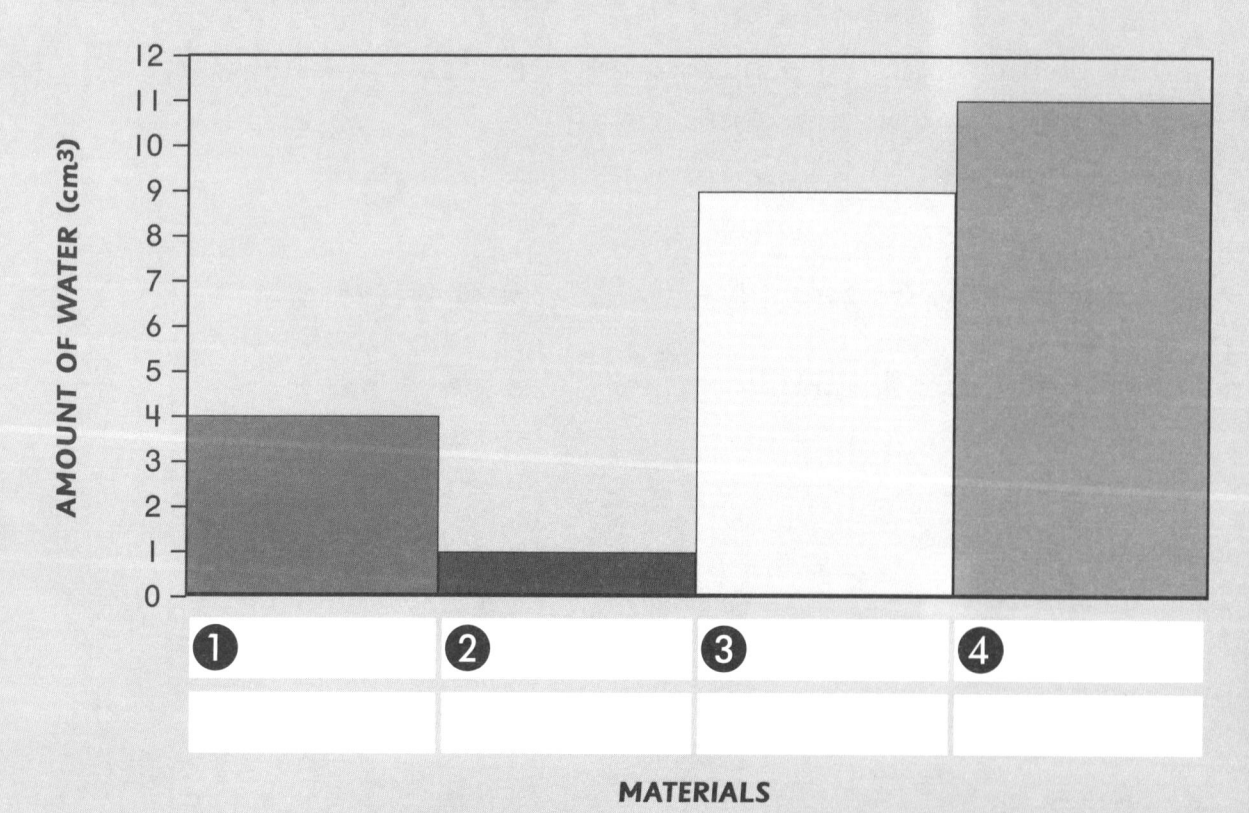

Write the name of each material, or mixture of materials, in the correct place on the chart.

MATERIALS AND THEIR PROPERTIES   TEST 10

Preserving food

Some children had a basket of raspberries. They wanted to find a way of preserving them and preventing them from going mouldy. They thought of four different ways:

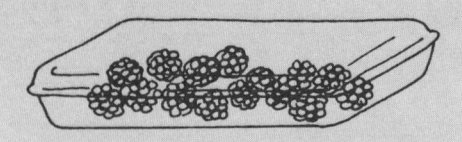

a putting them in a sealed container on a sunny windowsill

b putting them in a plastic container in the refrigerator

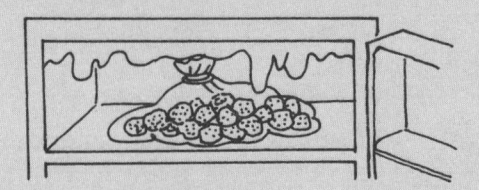

c putting them in a plastic bag in the freezer

d boiling them and sealing them in an airtight jar

5 Which do you think was the worst way of trying to keep the raspberries fresh?

6 Why?

Which two ways would have preserved the fruit for the longest time?

7

8

9 Why do frozen foods stay fresh?

10 Why do dried foods stay fresh?

11 Name another way of preserving food.

25

Physical Processes

TEST 11   Electrical circuits

Don made a simple electrical circuit using one bulb and one battery. He put different materials in the gap (①, ②) to try to complete the circuit.

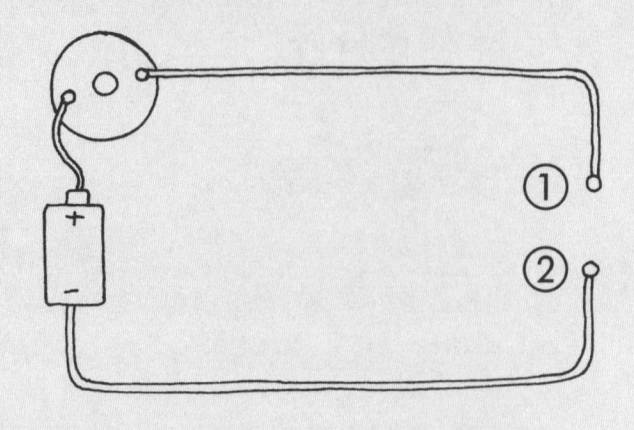

①-③ Which materials would conduct electricity and allow the bulb to light? Tick the boxes.

Material	Conductor	Non-conductor	Material	Conductor	Non-conductor
glass			fabric		
iron nail			tin foil		
steel knife			plastic comb		
wood			cardboard		

④ What is the special name for a material that does not allow electricity to pass through it?

An electromagnet

⑤-⑩ Draw an electromagnetic circuit. Use these materials.

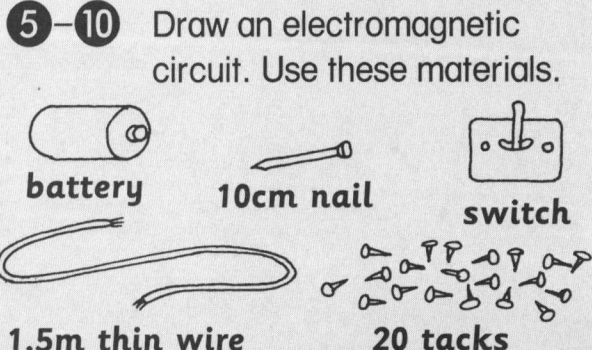

battery   10cm nail   switch

1.5m thin wire   20 tacks

PHYSICAL PROCESSES   TEST 11

Electricity and safety

Look at this picture.

Three things which could endanger life are happening in the picture.
What are they, and why are they so dangerous?

⑪ – ⑫
⑬ – ⑭
⑮ – ⑯

Insulators

A screwdriver used for electrical work needs a new handle.
Which of these materials would be unsuitable, and why?

⑰ – ⑱

**wood
plastic
rubber
steel**

27

Life Processes and Living Things/ Materials and their Properties/ Physical Processes

TEST 12   Changing materials

Some materials can be changed if they are:
- heated
- cooled
- put under pressure

① – ㉔ Tick the appropriate boxes for each of these materials.

MATERIALS

	Cake mix	Ice	Wax	Paper	Plasticine
is changed by heat					
is permanently changed by heat					
can be changed back					
is changed by cooling					
is permanently changed by cooling					
can be changed back					
is changed by pressure					
is permanently changed by pressure					
can be changed back					

PROPERTIES

On a very cold winter morning, the foil-covered top of a milk bottle may look like this.

— foil top
— milk bottle

㉕ – ㉗ Explain what has happened, and why.

LIFE PROCESSES/MATERIALS/PHYSICAL PROCESSES   TEST 12

Identifying living things

Here is a list of some of the characteristics of a plant and some of the characteristics of an animal.

a	reproduces using seeds or by rooting	f	has teeth and eyes
b	eats using its mouth	g	usually grows in the ground
c	can move from place to place using parts of its body	h	has petals and leaves
		i	hunts for its food
d	takes in nourishment through roots and leaves	j	attracts insects to help it pollinate
e	reproduces by mating with another of its own kind		

Here are two boxes, one containing a plant and one containing an animal. On each box are letters showing some of the characteristics of the living thing inside.

Match those letters to the statements above to identify what is in each box.

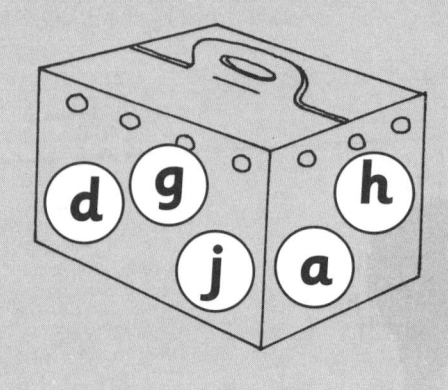

28 – 29   This box contains

30 – 31   This box contains

TEST 12   LIFE PROCESSES/MATERIALS/PHYSICAL PROCESSES

Sound

A submarine has a device that sends out and receives sound waves. How do the sailors in the submarine know when there are rocks ahead?

32 – 36 Draw what you think happens to the sound under water, and write about what happens.

37 The device used on a submarine for underwater listening is called _____.

38 The sound waves travel through _____.

A bat uses a similar location system to register an obstacle when it is flying in the dark.

39 – 42 Draw what happens when a bat uses this system.

43 This system is called _____.

LIFE PROCESSES/MATERIALS/PHYSICAL PROCESSES   TEST 12

Air

This experiment shows how air changes when it is heated.

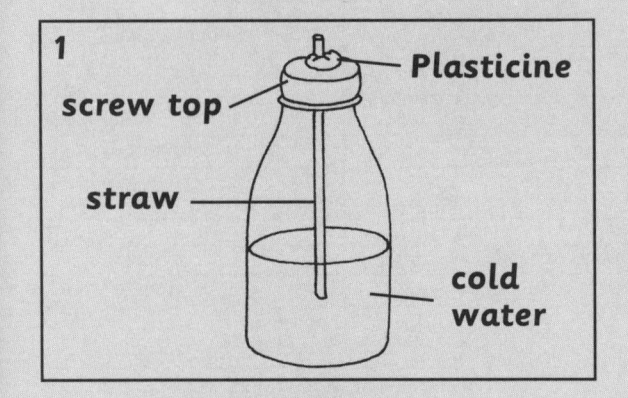

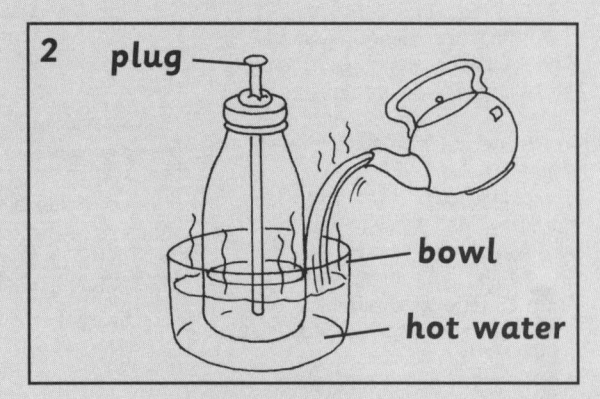

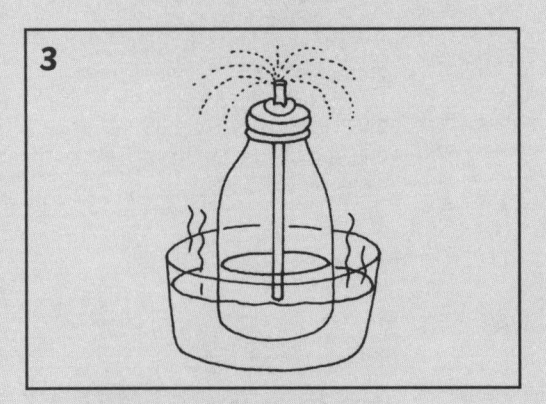

1 screw top — Plasticine — straw — cold water

2 plug — bowl — hot water

3

44 – 46 What has happened to make the water do this?

This experiment shows how air changes when it is cooled.

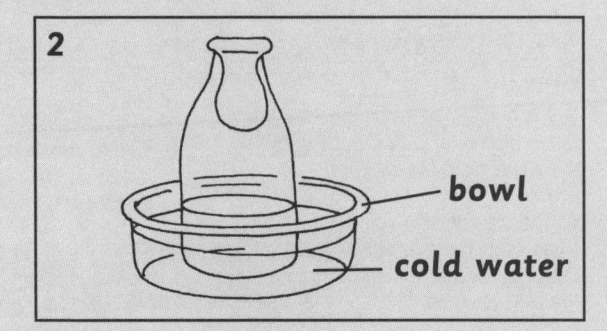

1 balloon — hot water

2 bowl — cold water

47 – 49 What has happened to make the balloon do this?

ANSWERS

TEST 1
1 non-living 2 living
3 non-living 4 non-living
5 living 6 living 7 non-living
8 living 9 non-living
10 non-living 11 non-living
12 non-living 13 non-living
14 non-living
15 – 20 Accept any 3 of the following, or any similar answers:
The plants and animals all need air.
The plants give out oxygen into the water. The animals take it in.
The plants and animals all need water.
The plants and animals all need the hard non-living things to give structure to their world.
21 the sun 22 the kestrel
23 – 25 The nuts and seeds feed the mice and voles which the kestrel needs for its food.
26 – 28 The consumers would either starve if the producers died, or be poisoned by eating them.

TEST 2
1 – 12 Award a point for each logical answer.
13 – 16 sugar, salt, instant coffee, icing sugar
17 It would (begin to) melt.
18 It would not change / would get warmer.
19 It would (begin to) melt.
20 It would (begin to) melt.
21 It would (begin to) melt.
22 It would get warmer.
23 – 27 Put the mixture in a jug of warm water, and stir until the sugar has dissolved. Pass the mixture through a fine sieve to collect the gravel, allowing the sugary water to collect in a container below.

TEST 3
1 – 3 Yes, by spreading its weight out into a flat disc or a boat shape.
4 – 5 air pressure and water pressure
6 The drum's skin vibrates.
7 by putting sand, rice or peas on the drum and watching them jump as the skin vibrates
8 air
9 c
10 – 12

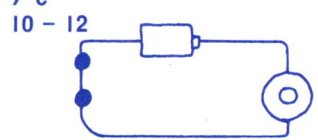

13 Yes
14 – 15 because like poles repel each other

TEST 4
1 ☼ 2 ☼ 3 ☼

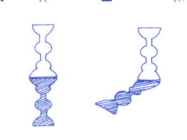

TEST 6
1 – 16

	Solid	Liquid	Gas	Remarks
has a shape of its own	✔			
keeps this shape	✔			
can be poured	✔*	✔		*e.g. sand, flour, sugar
finds its own level	✔*	✔		*e.g. sand, flour, sugar
can be squashed into a smaller space	✔*			*e.g. a sponge, fabric
floats above ground			✔	
falls to the ground when dropped	✔	✔		
flows through a tube	✔*	✔	✔	*e.g. sand, flour, sugar
can be transparent / translucent or opaque	✔	✔	✔	

4 winter 5 summer
6 Days are longer in summer.
7 – 9 Accept any 3 of the following: trees, branches, leaves, grass, clouds, smoke, curtain, kite, balloon, washing, flowers, hair
10 b
11 because it has a greater surface area to offer resistance to the air
12 by smoothing it flat
13 – 15

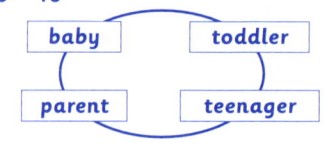

baby — toddler
parent — teenager

16 Smoking can cause breathlessness, heart disease and lung cancer.
17 You can breathe in their smoke (passive smoking).
18 wool
19 because the heat was able to escape from the egg
20 because the layers trap warm air between them

TEST 5
1 brain 2 lungs 3 heart
4 kidneys 5 stomach
6 – 8 sleeping, because the body is at its most relaxed
running, because the body is using a lot of energy and the heart has to pump more blood round
9 cactus 10 tree 11 rose
12 seaweed 13 buttercup
14 moss 15 bulrush

16 water 17 heat 18 light
19 no growth
20 poor, spindly growth
21 slow, stunted growth

17 water 18 by freezing it into ice
19 by boiling it into steam
20 Minimart 21 Tyson's
22 at the bottom or at the handle
23 Tyson's and Asdec
24 They could make bags which don't break when carrying weights of up to 10 kg.

TEST 7
1 – 4 This is the most likely arrangement:

Surface	Distance travelled
smooth wooden floor	5 m
short grass	25 cm
deep-pile carpet	2 cm
smooth PE mat	1.5 m
rough concrete path	20 cm
soil	12 cm

5 friction 6 deep-pile carpet
7 smooth wooden floor 8 gravity
9 – 13 The heavier car would (probably) travel further, because its greater weight would give it more thrust / impetus.
14 because the Earth is between the Sun and the Moon and is casting a shadow on the Moon
15 an eclipse 16 Earth
17 Earth 18 Earth 19 night
20

32